Life Begins When You Choose

Compiled by Joyce Gbeleyi

Onwards and Upwards Publishers

Berkeley House
11 Nightingale Crescent
Leatherhead
Surrey
KT24 6PD
United Kingdom

www.onwardsandupwards.org

Printed in the UK by 4edge Limited.

ISBN: 978-1-911086-01-7
Typeface: Sabon LT
Graphic design: LM Graphic Design

About the Editor.

Joyce was born in Leeds, West Yorkshire to Nigerian parents with three other siblings. She was brought up with Christian values, but the family split up when she was a young child.

She married at the age of twenty and enjoyed many adventures with her husband Olu, as well as family reconciliations. But a further ten years passed before she committed her life to Jesus. At that time Joyce and Olu had two daughters, Sarah and Maria, whom Joyce looked after while Olu was fully involved in Nigerian politics. During those times, Joyce learned about God's provision, with the help of devoted Christian colleagues at the literacy charity for which she worked.

Later, Joyce and her daughters spent time living in Nigeria to support Olu after his successful election into the Ogun State House of Assembly and selection as Deputy Speaker. Then they were blessed with a son, Simon, and relocated to Manchester.

Now at the age of fifty, Joyce is keen to share with others the lessons learned from her life experiences through a mature Christian lens. She is currently studying Kingdom Theology at Westminster Theological Centre (WTC) and is a member of Ivy Church, Manchester.

Endorsements

Before I arrived as Senior Leader at Ivy Church, a prophecy was given many years beforehand. A visiting speaker said he felt that three significant movements would happen in this church and from it, which would cause it to be a church of significant impact for the nation and the nations.

Movement one would be that it would galvanise people for prayer and unity on mission. That has happened and continues to happen as Ivy plants churches and encourages prayer and unity via NewThing as well as through a number of other partnerships such as Redeeming Our Communities.

The second movement would be that from Ivy many women would rise up to their full inheritance in the Kingdom and some of them would have ministries of major impact – more so even than the men in the fellowship. The phrase that was used was that these women would "come out of hiding and step out into the open" and I believe that this book is part fulfilment of that prophecy in our time.

The third movement, which remains an exciting one for me, spoke of more and more churches being planted in different places around this city and beyond. As an entrepreneurial city, Manchester people think differently and start things which others say can't be done. I'm privileged to lead a church where people of all backgrounds, races, ages and stages minister in the power of the Spirit with a confidence in the gospel regardless of gender.

The stories of life transformation and how those changed lives are changing the lives of others, contained within these pages, will, I'm sure, thrill and inspire you as they do me that the best is yet to come!

Anthony Delaney
Leader, Ivy Churches

Joyce looks at eleven ordinary women, shares an honest account of their lives and the result is inspiring.

The dictionary defines 'ordinary' as "of no exceptional ability, degree, or quality; average" but we find that with God, exceptional things can happen when we trust Him.

Joyce has captured this well as she lives this way herself. I am delighted to recommend her book to you.

Debra Green OBE
CEO of Redeeming Our Communities

Publisher's Note

The people, places, courses and events referred to in this book will be familiar to regular attenders of Ivy Church in Manchester. To find out more about the church, please visit their website at:

www.ivychurch.org.

Contents

INTRODUCTION

The impetus for the writing of this book came from a combination of sources, not least of which was the sudden realisation that I would turn fifty in 2016!

There was also Neil T. Anderson's life-changing 'Freedom in Christ' (FIC) course presented by Steve Goss. I first enquired about it in November 2014. At that time, I did not know how I could arrange childcare for Simon, our youngest. But from the moment I received David Challis's welcome email on 1st January, 2015, in which he stated that the FIC team "are going to be praying for you over these next few weeks that it is a significant time for you and that any schemes the enemy might have to put you off will be frustrated", I knew that there was no turning back and that God would take control. Amongst many things, the FIC course taught me to recognise that eternal life begins here on earth through Jesus Christ. This realisation brought me to understand my true commission and motivated me to find a way to bear fruit by aspiring to specific 'godly desires', which we reflected on in groups during session 12, entitled 'Where Are You Heading?'

Around the same time, as a church we were studying Rick Warren's 'Transformation' series in the Kingsway morning sermons and again in Grow Groups mid-week. My attention was drawn to Romans 12:1:

> *Therefore, I urge you, brothers and sisters, in view of God's mercy, to offer your bodies as a living sacrifice, holy and pleasing to God – this is your true and proper worship.*

During the series, I came to understand what the "Therefore" was there for: God's mercy, to which I needed to respond by being "transformed by the renewing of [my] mind" (Romans 12:2).

Then on Friday 20th March, a day remembered for its lunar eclipse, I was late in attending some workshops at Manchester Town Hall because I was feeling unwell. Yet no sooner had I found a seat than I was transfixed by the guest speaker, Dr Peter Hawkins, who delivered a thought-provoking icebreaker entitled 'No Regrets on Sunday'. His message challenged everyone present to do what they enjoyed and were passionate about so that when death took us, we would regret nothing. *Well, that shook me up!* So there and then I spoke out to the person sitting next to me, who just happened to be Andy Ashford from Ivy, and said, "I'm going to be a Life Coach," which I had been considering in a secular sense for a year, but thought I was not ready…

The final catalyst came on Sunday 22nd March, 2015, at Ivy Kingsway, when Anthony Delaney was speaking on 'Transforming Relationships' and the fears that ruin relationships. The aspect that deeply resonated with me was Anthony's comment that women were being crushed around the world due to "the battle of the sexes where women always lose and lose out", which started from the fall of Adam and Eve. That statement rang in my head over and over that afternoon while I was ironing my son's school uniform, and then I heard an inner voice asking me what I was going to do about it.

I carefully placed the iron to rest, while I processed what was happening and where this voice was coming from. Before I could stop myself, I had picked up my phone and hurriedly composed and sent an email to Anthony, explaining the concept of the book I was feeling called to write about Ivy Women and the calling I was feeling to become a Life Coach for Christian women.

Unfortunately, I later discovered on receiving his response that I had addressed Anthony as Andy in my email! But he was gracious enough not to refer to it, and instead gave me some much needed encouragement and useful leads of Ivy women to consult with.

The rest, as they say, is HIS story.

So please join me in accepting the challenge to be *excellent* in doing a *new thing* for Christ. I pray that by reading the spiritual journeys of these eleven Ivy women you will find your voice and recapture your dreams to excel.

Remain blessed!

Joyce Gbeleyi

KERRYANNE HARRISON

Age:	*39*
Family:	*Single parent with two sons*
Started at Ivy:	*2012*
Choice of beverage:	*Skinny latte*

I am the eldest of four children and come from a loving family that did not go to church except for weddings and funerals. I was an atheist.

I was brought up to be quite independent and encouraged to do my own thing. So I left home at seventeen – an early age, I now realise. I was far too young to cope socially and emotionally, and obviously not ready for it, but my mum and dad had separated in my late teens and I just decided it was better for me to be living by myself.

From a young age I always wanted to be independent and to be challenged, because of my strong work ethic. So since the age of about thirteen, when I started my first paper round, I have always had a job.

I had a little flat and worked to earn money. After finishing school, I went to college and studied Beauty Therapy, but I didn't really like it. I don't know why; it just wasn't enough for me. The reason I chose to study Beauty Therapy was because I didn't want to undertake an academic style of course.

In 1999, when I was twenty-two, I decided to go back to university. So as a mature student, I decided to take an access course, and was accepted into Manchester University. In 2000 I started a degree in Criminology and Sociology, whilst still working practically full-time in the evenings and weekends; so it was quite full on! I was really passionate about doing this course and quite determined.

Then unexpectedly, just as I started my third year of study and at the age of twenty-six, I became pregnant with my first child. At six months I became really quite ill. I was diagnosed on Christmas Eve, 2002, with what they told me was a brain haemorrhage. Well, it wasn't... Then after a few more days and a few more tests they told me that I had a tumour on my pituitary gland – not a cancerous tumour, but they thought it was growing and that I would need to have surgery. It never turned out like that, but I did have to go to Christie Hospital for a long time – during my pregnancy and for a couple of years after.

I separated from my partner when things weren't working out. But then a funny thing happened; we started getting on great when we were not living as a family unit. So we got back together. My partner was, and still is, brilliant with the boys, but our relationship was not so great; so we split up again shortly after the birth of my second child. I found myself on my own with two young children.

When I separated from my partner, my youngest child was nine months old and my eldest was coming up for five years. It was probably the hardest period that I have been through in my life. Just physically... They were so little and they need you so much. I felt like the walking dead most of the time.

I had worked for Trafford Social Services but now trained as a Teaching Assistant. I was thirty-two and my life revolved around the boys (and has continued to do so for a very long time). I needed a job that fitted in around them. Over a period of years, I became depressed. I fought it for a long time but when it finally did get me, it really floored me for about eighteen months. My job as a Teaching Assistant is rewarding and I like it – I always try to do it well – but I only do it because it fits in well around my boys.

People constantly asked, "When are you going to meet somebody? Come on, you've been on your own for ages." But I didn't want to meet anybody; I was happy being on my own and didn't want to embark on another unhappy relationship.

I had been on a night out to celebrate a friend's birthday. At this point I had been on my own looking after my boys for four and a half years. Again my 'singleness' was the main topic of conversation from my well-meaning friends who wanted to see me in a relationship. On my way home in the taxi that night I thought, "Why do people do this? Why do people want these things that I don't want for myself?"

Then, very suddenly, in the back of a taxi, an atmosphere of peace came over me and I heard myself say, "Go home, you are fine. I am going to look after you. You don't need for anything. You have got healthy children, a lovely home, friends and family. When the time is right, you will know it, and when that right person is there for you,

you will not ever have to question it. You will be able to love and you will be able to trust. Just go home for now and do what you want to do."

I was amazed. "Wow, that's good thinking Kerry!" I congratulated myself. It wasn't just the words; I felt *joy!* It was three o'clock in the morning and I felt so *happy;* I almost skipped out of the taxi! I went into my house and off to bed knowing that I was different.

In the morning my friend phoned me. "Becky, Becky!" I said to her, excitedly. "The weirdest thing happened to me in a taxi last night..." I recounted the story to her and then added, "Do you know, I don't know what's happened to me but I've changed!"

"What do you mean?" Becky asked.

"I don't know, but I've changed!" I insisted. "I don't know how I feel, Becky... I feel like a *completely different person.* But what I do know is, not everybody is going to like this."

Now, looking back, I know exactly what that meant, but at that point I had no idea! I had never even picked up a bible, yet I had had my first encounter of the Holy Spirit there in the back of the taxi.

Later that Saturday morning, I told my aunty what had happened. We were out for a coffee. Again I simply acknowledged, "I'm different."

On the following Monday I had arranged for someone to come and decorate my house but he could not do it. He came round to ask me if it was okay for his son to do it instead. He also told me that his son used to have a bad reputation but had changed. So, for three days this man was in my house and he talked endlessly about God. He told me how God had turned his life around. He would list all the things he didn't do anymore, and I would answer that I didn't do them either but I wasn't a Christian!

I met someone who had known this man when he was a boy at school. He said the man had been very different back then; he used to be in trouble a lot. I started to ask myself, *what if?* What if there's something more to it? There's no way he could just wake up and change completely.

The workman left me a small copy of the Gospel of John. I started reading it, but it felt like I was *drinking* it. I found myself wanting to go to bed early so that I could read it and have a bit of time to myself.

I thought, "This is really strange! Why am I thinking about the possibility of there being a God and wanting to read the Bible?"

As you will recall, I was not from a family that regularly went to church; we were brought up with our own free will to make our own decisions. My father was educated by Catholic nuns, and it had left him with a very negative impression of God and religion. As for me, I was set in my atheism and thought that people who believed in God were crackers! I couldn't understand how people could believe in all that.

In September, I went to the first Ivy Church service after the summer – and it was very scary. I didn't want to talk to anyone. I just wanted to sit at the back. I came with a friend; she was a Catholic and she said, "I'm going to come with you. We'll sit near the back. Don't worry, if anybody does ask you anything, I will be able to answer some of the questions." So I came in and I hid – but looking at all the people, I thought, "Well, they look really normal."

They looked really normal... like me, or my family or my friends. Then the worship started and everyone stood up and – oh, my word! Anthony Delaney's sermon that day was about King Solomon. I thought, "I'm not going to understand a word of this," but I completely understood the whole of his talk.

As I walked out of the meeting that day, I found myself thinking, "I don't know what it is you've got, but *I want that!* That's what I want! I need that!" From that time, I never stopped going to church.

I decided to do the Alpha course in October, which I did with Andy and Michelle Hawthorne. "Why am I doing this?" I wondered. "I don't even believe in God." Week after week I had the same thought, yet every Monday for two months I would want to go again.

Ridiculous things began to happen and I would think, "That was from God! That was from God!" I started opening up to people and I told my friends and family I had started going to church! So that was it – I had begun my journey with God.

At the end of the Alpha course, Andy said I needed to get baptised. I disagreed but he insisted, "Yes, you really do." So I said, "Okay then, yes, I will." And that was the crunch for me because then I had to go and see my dad and tell him I was going to get baptised. I think he knew I was going to church, but he didn't realise how serious I was.

I can't put into words what a difference getting baptised has made to me. The day of the baptism was 2nd December, 2012. The enemy seemed to be 'all over me' – I felt sick, I couldn't eat, I couldn't think, I was making mistakes, doing all the wrong things. I went for lunch with Michelle and confirmed to Anthony I would get baptised, but explained that I couldn't speak in front of the church. I thought he would say, "Oh, that's all right, you don't really have to." But he just looked at me and said, "Well, you're doing it and you're going to go out and you're going to say where, why and when!"

Inside I was shouting, "I can't, I can't," and for the rest of the day I was in quite a state. I phoned the woman leading the service, Debra, and was almost hysterical insisting I really did want to get baptised but couldn't stand up in front of people.

She said, "Don't worry, there's loads of you!" (Apparently, it was the biggest baptism service Debra had ever led. In the end there were about twenty people who were getting baptised.) "We'll say that we're over-running and that there's not enough time for you to speak." So we hatched a little plan.

My mum, dad, my two closest friends, my brothers and my sister were coming. So the immediate and most important people in my life were going to be there watching me. But as I was sitting in the service, waiting and thinking I couldn't go up, a peace came over me and I heard a kind of voice saying, "Of course you can. You're going to stand up and share exactly what's happened to you. Also your family are here and you're going to tell them who you were, who you are now, and what has happened."

When my turn came, I stood up and Debra said, "This is Kerryanne – but we're out of time."

"No!" I blurted out. "I want to speak!"

I must have spoken for about fifteen minutes. I couldn't stop. That was the Holy Spirit, because I didn't know half the words that were coming out of my mouth – it was just amazing. Then I got baptised.

Since then, many things have happened in my family, things like people being very sick. It was as if I was being prepared to be a rock! It's as if everything just washed over me whereas before I would have been swept along with it. But that doesn't happen to me anymore.

I had felt really old at thirty-six when I was baptised and started to go to church. I had felt drained and washed out. Life had been really hard. But it was like becoming refreshed; I realised I was not so old and that I could do many things. I realised that in my workplace I was there for a reason. Although I had thought about leaving on a number of occasions, I never could, and I now realised why that was. I had a sense of 'blooming where you're planted'. It was like God was saying, "This is where I've planted you; go and do what you need to do, and when your time is up, I will repot you somewhere else." And so even my attitude to my job has been much more gracious and I get more satisfaction from it.

My relationship with my children, which at times had been difficult, is so much better than it was. I can parent much better. God has shown me so much grace and love when I have not been a very nice or loving person to others. He has shown me that's how to bring out the best in people. People thrive when they experience unconditional love. So that's what I have to do with my children. We still have off days, but in general it is much more chilled.

For three years now I have been getting to grips with a life that was very new to me. When I first started coming to church there was a bit of awkwardness. I asked God to help me. Fortunately, Ivy being the place it is, lots of people came to me and supported me. After a few weeks I became more comfortable

Last year, at the school where I have been working for five years, I felt God telling me it was time to move on. But I will be leaving it on a positive note, whereas a few years ago I might have left for the wrong reasons and in my own timing.

Suddenly now I feel like the Lord is saying, *"It's your time now."* Not that the time looking after my children has not been valuable but God has shown me that so far I have focused fully on being a mum and now he will give me the capacity to do even more. I have lived for a very long time on a very small wage. It's not just a financial struggle, it can be a burden because you feel so constrained. Yet God has always provided.

There were elements of my personality which I saw as weaknesses, such as being too sensitive or too emotional, worrying about people too much. But now I know that it can be a calling. I've been given a gift of compassion and empathy, and I now know that the Lord is telling me to 'let my light shine'. I now realise that what I thought were weaknesses are actually my strengths.

I met with Anthony Delaney and told him that I didn't know if I was really doing the right thing but I did feel I was listening to God. I felt as if I needed to relinquish where I was in order for other things to open up. When you first have a plant in your garden or in your planter, at first it's brilliant; it grows and grows and grows. But you have to prune it and cut off the dead heads and the dead wood or else it won't flourish again. The last piece of dead wood from my past has gone and I am going forward to bear fruit.

So I feel more confident now than I think I have ever done in my life: confident in my own abilities; confident in what God wants me to do and what I am capable of.

I work with Ivy Kids, where we did a brilliant training series called 'Story Line'. The premise of Story Line is that you envision the ending/goal and you work backwards from where you want to get to, filling in the gaps in between, instead of living retrospectively, which is what we normally do. "What's your goal? What do you want it to be? What do you want it to look like, and how are you going to get there?" We asked these questions. Then we did an Encounter series, in which we wanted the children to be as prophetic as they could be and listen out for God's word.

The Lord led me to a tunnel on an embankment in my Encounter vision. I was on a beach and I looked through the tunnel. The beach through the tunnel was whiter and the sea was bluer. But I said, "This beach is fine; I'm fine over here."

The Lord said, "I want for you what's over there; it's the same but better."

When I tell people that I am leaving my current job and they ask what I will do, I say I will trust the Lord.

I have enrolled on the WTC Graduate Diploma and I am waiting on the Lord for the provision. If it's God's plan for me to do it, then I trust in Him that He will provide and open all the necessary doors for it to happen.

Onwards and upwards!

CRYSTAL BERRIDGE

Age:	*44*
Family:	*Married with two children*
Started at Ivy:	*2013*
Choice of beverage:	*Skinny Americano (decaf)*

I started a Christian charity called Hampers of Hope before I began to get involved at Ivy. The charity had been going for about eighteen months when I became a church member, together with my husband Lee and my two children, William (now seven) and Helena (now six).

I started the poverty relief charity because of something that happened at a Grow Group meeting at my previous church. A certain lady there said to me, "I don't really want to tell you this..." She was embarrassed; it turned out she had been feeding another lady in church and had ended up not having enough food to support her own family because she was helping her friend.

My background has nothing to do with foodbanks or relieving poverty. My background is in Strategic Marketing and Marketing Management. Lee and I run our own property business. So I knew nothing about foodbanks at the time; all I could do was to give her some money. However, at that moment God inspired me to do something about the situation. He revealed to me the whole idea right then. To be honest, I don't even know what happened during the rest of the Grow Group because I was caught up with this new idea. I went from the meeting to my car, phoned Lee and said, "We need to talk!"

We met at the Trafford Shopping Centre for coffee and I explained that I felt God was asking me to do something about local people's food poverty. "I want to start collecting food for Christmas hampers."

He said, "We might do about twenty – or twenty-five." I had a hundred in my mind, but decided not to tell him so that I wouldn't scare him too much!

This was in October 2011. I asked friends and local churches that I knew of to start collecting food. In the end, we delivered 101 hampers for Christmas 2011 and fed around 250 people.

I live in Cheshire. A lot of people think it is very affluent there – and it is, but there is also a great deal of poverty.

Once the Christmas project was over, I realised that half of those 250 people were children. At the time I had two children aged one and three so I felt deeply moved. God moves us through our hearts, doesn't he? And so I felt moved with compassion to start a charity called Hampers of Hope. I needed to learn about foodbanks so I started doing my homework!

At the time, I was going to a small church, and Hampers of Hope started gathering momentum with lots of people supporting it. My neighbours and friends started raising money. You have to raise £5,000 to start a registered charity and they helped me. The whole thing began to snowball. It was still a *little* snowball at the time but as it gathered momentum, it started to affect people in our church who felt inspired to join in. However, the charity work shifted the focus of some people away from what the church leaders wanted and so a conflict started to develop. It wasn't one that I wanted but it was there. It was a difficult situation being a woman dealing with church leaders who were all men. But I belonged to a wonderful Grow Group of encouraging women and they gave me much needed support, encouragement and prayer.

It was during this time that Lee attended a Message Business Network event. He phoned me and said, "I'm having a coffee with a person called Frank Green."

I replied, "Aren't we too busy? Why are you having coffee?"

But it was a God moment! Frank mentioned that his wife Debra was involved in charity work, helping in the community, and Lee suggested that I speak to her. Debra emailed me to meet for a coffee. I agreed.

Before meeting her, I Googled her name. What I found out shocked me. "Do you know who Debra Green is?" I exclaimed to Lee. "She only runs a national charity![1] And she is inviting me for coffee!"

We met and she told me of the benefits of being part of a church with a "big vision". I left the meeting encouraged but questioning whether I was in the right church for me and my family. The idea of

---

[1] Redeeming Our Communities

leaving resonated with me as I felt limited where I was. At the same time, I loved my church and particularly my Grow Group; they were like family to me and had supported me right from the start of the charity.

Eventually, God called us to Ivy. I went to Ivy Didsbury on a Sunday night and heard Anthony Delaney speak. He was full of faith. I have faith but he has *great* faith! We took the kids. Dave Hill, the children's worker, took a custard pie in the face and the kids loved it. They wanted to go to the "custard pie church".

I know now why we were called to Ivy – because Anthony is a leader of leaders. He once said to me that part of his job is to be a "cheerleader" for all the people who are out there working for God – and he's really good at that. We have found inspirational leaders who head up local, national and international ministries at Ivy. This is really empowering for us and others who are also leading businesses and ministries.

I felt excited because here many people are attempting to do something great for God, changing their worlds for the better. You start speaking to people and listen to their stories and you think, "God's doing amazing work here." It's really encouraging and very inspirational.

Ivy's a really great place to be, because you feel supported and built up when you're having your down moments; you can go to church and feel empowered again. So many of us at Ivy are on the front line, going out into the communities where people are in need in one way or another; Ivy is somewhere where people like that can go to feel empowered and inspired.

During my time at Ivy, the charity has grown beyond recognition. It now covers the whole of North-East Cheshire and we have over eighty volunteers going out almost every day of the year helping people. We have expanded the scope of Hampers of Hope dramatically. It has become a charity focused on relieving poverty in every way that it can, not just a foodbank but with job clubs, money management courses and Hope Centres in four locations. These centres have been an amazing success. We are seeing people's lives changed dramatically for the good and people finding their way back to God. We plan to open more centres until there is one in each location where we feed people in Cheshire. It is amazing what you can do when you feel supported by your church family!

One thing that I have been looking for is a mentor but this has been hard to find. In many churches men in leadership are being mentored, but not women. It may be because most church leaders are male and understandably don't want to risk being compromised. I asked Anthony what the plan was for mentoring women in leadership at Ivy and he suggested I start something. That is how Christian Women in Leadership was born. The group has been going for four months at this point and there are now about thirty of us meeting once a month. We meet to learn from each other and invite guest speakers to learn from and be encouraged and inspired by. We are in the beginnings of this movement and only God knows where it will go!

One thing that I have learned at Ivy is to "just go for it". If it is what God wants, it will grow, and if it doesn't, try something new. God brought me and my family to Ivy. I am so glad because I feel encouraged and inspired by the vision and by the Ivy members who share the same heart to reach people for Jesus.

Onwards and upwards!

TRACY MCCORMICK

Age:	*49*
Family:	*Married with two children*
Started at Ivy:	*2007*
Choice of beverage:	*Decaf skinny latte*

I was adopted into a loving family when I was just eight days old. My parents already had an adopted son aged eight; then, when I was four years old, they had a natural child.

With that diversity came problems. Although it all looked very nice, my mother had mental health problems. Mine were very rigid, older parents; they had fostered for a long time. My adoptive brother hated me – and their natural child didn't particularly want me either. Even though the adoption papers emphasize that the older boy loved me and wanted me, it didn't happen that way. There was a lot of damage done and we don't have a relationship anymore – but God rescued me through a lot of that.

When I got to the age of eight, my father had a job transfer to South Africa, so we all packed up the house and went over there. I think it was my saving grace because it gave us a whole new life, a new outlet and the opportunity to meet lots of people.

My mum and dad would go to the Church of England services after just having had a horrendous row and I would say, "Don't cry, Mummy." She'd put her head down, and it would be a real farce. But inside me I always knew that there was someone else who loved me because I felt so unloved, so trapped. I didn't really exist. I was just in the middle of this awful situation, and school was not much better.

When I went to church, even though they had their big long dresses and the bells and incense and everything, I found an essence of God. There was something that was more than me. When I sang my little songs at school, it made my home life bearable.

In South Africa, we shared a hotel with another couple who spent quite a lot of time talking to my parents. When I was about eleven or twelve they took us to a Baptist church and Youth With A Mission (YWAM) which was the mission that had come to the church.

At the YWAM event I asked Jesus to come into my life. There was a massive altar call. I thought, "I need to go forward," but I was too shy. Then I realised I was already standing up and feeling great – so I just walked to the front. I thought I was just going to get into their wagon and have a wonderful life in America – at the age of eleven! – but of course it didn't happen that way.

Life trundled on. I spent 1978 to 1980 in England but then returned to South Africa. There I went to a huge Baptist church called Rhema. (Rhema is Ray McCauley's church in Johannesburg.) My mum had asked me to come with her. She got saved and I went forward with her, but I got baptized with the Holy Spirit and started speaking in tongues. During that time people were getting healed and getting out of wheelchairs. Lots of incredible things were happening and I felt transformed. I was able to reach out and love, and be loved. I was able to hug people. And my life was changed.

My dad wasn't saved yet so we were still praying for him. I joined the sister church which was our local connection to the main church and I went to the youth club. And then I hit my late teens...

I had trained to be a hairdresser at sixteen and had gone into the workplace. It was an industry that was dominated by homosexuality and drug abuse. All sorts of things were going on, and instead of my youth leader saying, "Right, well we'll pray through these things. We'll make sure you're okay working within that," it was, "Stay away, don't talk to them."

I had a rebellious spirit; it didn't work for me like that. So, boy, did I go for it! I went into it hook, line and sinker and fell into the whole 'living in the city'. I was an amphetamine user, I had anorexia and I left home when I was eighteen. I was drinking like never before and then turning up for work. I fought with my parents and it was just crazy, crazy, crazy. I used the excuse that because my dad wasn't saved I didn't have to come under his roof.

One day I found myself standing in front of my window. I'd had boyfriends abusing me and I'd gone through horrendous abuse at one particular boyfriend's hands. I was ready. I was ready to turn it all in! I was standing at the window of my flat and I had put a record on, a

Christian record. The words seemed to be directed at me, and I knew it was the Holy Spirit saying to me, "It's not your time, it's not your time now, it's not your time." So I stood there for a moment. Then I stepped back on to the bed. "Right, this is it."

Following that, for about six months, my old youth friends kept coming into my place of work. "We love you! We want you back! We love you!" I was about six-and-a-half stone, my uniform was hanging off my back and I was completely 'off my face' most of the time. But they just embraced me wholeheartedly. They would come one at a time and then I would call my mum and shout, "You sent them! I'm living this life and I'm happy."

They invited me down to a service one evening and I thought, "Oh well, I might as well go." We were meeting in a tent at the time because in Johannesburg we had Apartheid and we had to find land that would accommodate a multiracial congregation. (Rhema was the first multiracial church that embraced all races.) So we had to find land where we could all be together from different races; it covered the whole cast: Chinese, Lebanese etc. But all we could put on the land was a big tent. My friends were waiting and they had saved my seat where I'd always sat between my friends. I prayed, "Lord, I want you back in my life!" The first thing I did was speak in tongues again for the first time in a couple of years. It took me by surprise! God reminded me, "I give good gifts and I don't take them away."[2]

I had a prophetic gifting. When I researched and found my birth parents I discovered I was a Roma Gypsy and I did have a cult background in my youth. So I know God has saved me from that and then used the Holy Spirit to put my gifts into heavenly hands.

I took charge of several youth clubs; I also ran an over-eighteen youth club because there were many undiscipled young people.

Then in 1987 my dad decided that we were "going home". He explained his reasons. We had had a lot of bereavements and family members dying. They had built a big home and done very well for themselves; they'd settled and life was very good. My brother had married and had children. And it was the right time.

I was living in a Christian Community with a couple of other girls and they were at bible college. I had a boyfriend and I had gone through a deep heart transformation and change, just relying on God

---

[2] See James 1:17

and asking Him to heal me. I told my parents that I wasn't going home with them – and it broke their hearts.

There was much anger and upset and my sister didn't want to go either. She said, "If you don't go, I won't go." But she was only fifteen at the time. I told her she had no choice.

At that time, I felt a heavy sorrow. I'm the kind of person who sobs in the shower. I was just sobbing and sobbing, but I couldn't understand why. So I went to my bible for answers and God showed me the picture of Mary and Joseph carrying Jesus. He impressed on me, "You might have been a child of adoption, you might have gone through things, you might have gone through abuse as a child, but *I chose these parents* for you." When I found my birth mother, she said, "I could have left you in a telephone box and you could have been put in foster care. If it had been a year later, you could have been aborted because that came in in 1967." I felt God telling me that he had watched over my life and it was time to go – to my new mission field. I needed to go home to England. That is where I belonged and I needed to come under the covering of my parents for a new ministry.

My dad came to work to check up on me one day. I had just finished for the day and he stood at the reception. "Right," he said, "I am going to get these tickets."

"Right," I replied, "I am coming home."

He sobbed and sobbed – laughter and cooing – and this all happened right in the middle of the salon with all my workmates. He said, "I'll see you later. I'll just go and get the tickets."

Within ten minutes he came back.

"What's happening?" I asked.

"We had booked our tickets but I hadn't got one for you," he told me. "The only seat that was left on the flight was the one next to your sister." My father had become a Christian by this point so he had been praying. God had kept that seat empty.

There was a great exodus out of South Africa around 1987 and flights were getting double-booked. When we got to the airport the plane was already *triple-booked,* so it was first come first served. If you bought a ticket, three different people had bought your seat. So when you got there with your seat number you might find it had been also sold to someone else and they would put you up in a hotel till the next day. There was chaos trying to get people out of the country.

We spent one night at the hotel. Then all my youth group turned up. I had already said goodbye to everyone – but now they all turned up again along with my best friend Charmeine. Her family were not Christians and we had prayed together for our fathers. Her family were very hostile to her being at bible college; she was my saving grace and a great friend. The Lord said to me, "Just have this time with Charmeine now; I've sent her to the airport." So we had half an hour and said everything we needed to say; we hugged and we loved.

Within six months of my return to England, Charmeine had a fatal car accident. I had been phoning her as there were no emails. Then one of my other friends phoned and I said, "How's everything? I feel uncomfortable; what's happening?" She told me that Charmeine had been in a car coming through an intersection. Lorries used to fly through our small town in South Africa. On this occasion, a lorry didn't stop at the light and it severed her car in half. She was just twenty-one.

I was devastated. But what a solace I got from her funeral a week later! All her family, including her father, her two brothers and her mum, knelt down at the side of her grave and gave their lives to the Lord. Her words kept coming to my mind: "I'd give my life to save my family; I'd give my life to see them change." I always hear the words of the song, "As the deer pants for the water, so my soul longs after you." That was her heart, as if her whole life was sold out for her family, and that really inspired me. I wanted to let my life resemble that and mean more than cars and houses and bank accounts; I wanted to let it mean family and people.

When people hurt me I used to self-harm and go into myself; rather than hit back I would take it out on myself. And so God started that journey in me and he said it was time to die to self and to get rid of that 'self' thing.

I met someone I liked called David through the receptionist at the hairdresser's – but he wasn't a Christian. So I put a 'fleece' out before God. "Right," I prayed, "I'm in this new country, I'm hanging round with these friends and her brother. If he's not saved in six months, then I need something to happen or I need to say goodbye." So I took David along to everything Christian. His family had no church background at all, and his parents were very 'anti'. They worked all over the country – all over the world, in fact – and he had been at home on his own from the age of eighteen. He was twenty-five when I met him and very independent.

So I took him to all sorts! At the Apollo Theatre there was a meeting called The Message that launched in 1989. The first thing I took him to in church was a wedding. A week later the bridegroom was tragically killed in a car accident. So the second thing I took him to was the funeral of the wedding party.

Everything was thrown at David to stop him being a Christian. In fact, it took a football injury on that final night. David asked God to heal him of his football injury *six months to the deadline I had set!*

I had planned to tell him that night that we had to split and was thinking, "Come on God! What's it going to take?" I'd already put the ground rules down. I don't believe in sex before marriage. I go to church and he was quite happy with that. But he wanted a break of his lifestyle and he said to God, "If you're real, heal this!" And so of course He did! And it freaked David out!

"What are you doing?" I asked.

"God's healed me!" he replied.

"So what did you say to God?"

He hesitated for a moment, a little embarrassed. He mumbled, "I'll believe in you! I'll ask you to come into my life if you heal me!" Then he panicked. "Take it back; I want it back, you're terrifying me!"

I laughed, "You've made a deal. That's it!"

So a certain someone went forward at the church meeting. He went up and gave his life to the Lord, and He got baptised with the Holy Spirit all in the same evening and he was absolutely 'drunk' in the Spirit!

He drove me home after the meeting. We pulled up outside my parents' home and I told him that this night was the night it was going to be over. That was about October, and by December we got engaged. A year and a half later we were married.

It was not easy because David parents were non-practising Catholics. They believed you were born a Catholic and you died a Catholic. So we had a very hostile reception from his family. However, one of the wonderful things that happened was that we went to Lincoln a month after he got saved to see his grandma. She said, "I thought something was funny because I've got all the grandchildren in the back room on the wall and last Sunday night your picture fell and smashed on the floor, and I wondered. You're a new man, aren't you, David?" It was her only grandson so something special happened there.

I have seen many of these significant things happen. We have run youth meetings together on the New Mills Estate. We have had children addicted to alcohol and drugs come to my parents' home. In addition to those outreach meetings I have been running a charity for eight years in Stockport called Stepping Stones, which runs like a coffee shop for drug addicts, alcoholics and the homeless.

I have always done voluntary work because my son has Asperger's. He wasn't diagnosed until he was nineteen so we'd been through 'hell and high water' and it's still ongoing. He's been mistaken by the police for being drunk and disorderly on the streets. He's been beaten up three times and hospitalised. He's been in a coma once. We've worked through drug addiction with him and alcoholism. It has been horrendous. He's twenty-three now and at the time of writing he's still not back at church. So we deal with that on a daily basis.

We moved from our home church to another church which had a great youth ministry. My daughter Fayth got saved there, which was great. I asked them about women's work but there was none. So a friend of mine called Andrea who works here at the Message told me about Ivy Church.

I went away for six months and went to Vine Life for a while, just a sabbatical to decide what to do. Do I just sit and do nothing, become stagnant and not use my gifts, or do I move on? I decided to move on.

Vine Life was amazing for me. They have a prophetic ministry which I loved. It was just a time of bathing in God, waiting day to day with faith. I simply allowed God to have His own control of my life. Even though you're married you still have your own relationship with God; you still have to work that out separately and together. So it took my husband a bit longer to work this through and my daughter longer still because she had many friends there who did not want her to move on to something new. And she struggled.

We moved to Ivy about seven years ago, about six months after Anthony Delaney had come; it was exactly what we needed at the time. It was small and local – we were living in Cheadle – and was everything we needed. It was family, it was love. My husband and I came together and then invited Fayth, who had heard about it. A couple of weeks later she came and said, "Right, that's it, I'm coming." So we came as a family, which was lovely. And we just grew from that; we went to

Denise Lamberth's Grow Group, which is really like a family with lots of love and protection.

My son was still having problems and I had a lot of help through the Grow Group. When police were knocking on the door and social workers were 'screaming' at me, my group helped me to draw close to God. I prayed, "I need your peace. I need to know your unconditional peace that has no limits."

And during that time of total turmoil, when the family was being turned upside down, God turned up. It wasn't about the church. It wasn't about the Bible (because I couldn't even read the Bible at that time). I was so desolate and felt abandoned, both physically and emotionally. But God showed up and helped me as I moved into Ivy.

For a while I was a Christians Against Poverty (CAP) befriender and then I trained as a debt coach. My husband's business had gone 'belly up' in 2000 and we had lost the house. In fact, we lost everything. We lived through horrendous times, so I always use that debt part of my life for CAP, because it is such an amazing charity.

As I was training to be a debt coach our landlord put the house up for sale and we looked at seven houses at least. By the time I went for my training in Leeds, we had nowhere to live. We had a week to move out of the house and nowhere to go. Our friends prayed for us and while I was away David texted and said he thought he'd found a place. It was in Wythenshawe, just up the road from Sharston. Our hopes were high. So I went and looked at it. It was just right.

My husband and I have always been pioneers and involved in church plants. Things were changing rapidly at Sharston. There was a Muslim lady coming and she was in the transition of getting saved; so we invited her to come.

We live on the estate and I belong to a Women of Influence African ministry, where they mentor you and show you that you have the authority of Christ in you. I found the African link helpful; I really needed the cultural encouragement and wanted to be involved in the lives of other women.

I now have much going on in my life and I am enjoying all of the many fruitful ways I can serve the Lord.

Onwards and upwards!

TRACEY SWEETMAN

Age: *45*
Family: *Single with one daughter*
Started at Ivy: *2014*
Choice of beverage: *Flat white coffee*

I had a friend from school whom I had known since I was eleven. We lost touch.

Several years later someone I worked with at Kendal's introduced me to the bible and Christianity, so I went with him and his wife for a little while to Kings Church. I met my friend again there, but I generally hid from her because I didn't want her to see me going to church. "What *am* I doing?" I thought. "She's a Christian – obviously!" But we both went our own way.

We met up again when I was going to a different church – and I did the same thing. We parted again but then met up a third time, and she introduced me to Ivy Church when they were meeting in the Forum.

I wasn't brought up as a Christian although I went to church for a bit. I didn't really 'get it', and I just thought that if I listened to the sermons and said I was a Christian, I'd get it. But I didn't.

Unfortunately, I left the church not long after meeting a man who became the father of my daughter. (She is now twenty-four.) After giving birth, I suffered with a lot of mental health problems. It started as postnatal depression which then led to clinical depression. I attempted suicide but found release through self-harm. I daily self-harmed for years – sometimes my arms, legs, throat, and even my face. I had urges to set fire to myself and hurt myself all the time.

I was very distressed, and in and out of a psychiatric unit for three years. My daughter went to live with my mum and stayed there from ages four to seven. For me, it was downhill from there. I ended up living with someone I met in a psychiatric unit and my life just continued to be destructive. I met someone from a church which turned out to be registered as a cult. This led to confusion because they told me they were "the way and the truth". While they were taking me to London to be baptised, a girl I knew from Kings Church stopped me on the bus and told me the truth. I believe God sent her there and saved me, but I became obsessed seeking all the news I could about this church through Manchester Library. I got into wrong relationships with men at this time.

Throughout those three years, my daughter was 'coming backwards and forwards' with me. I had been smoking cannabis, hearing voices, and things weren't looking good with the depression. I started to feel a bit better again so I went to church for a bit and took my daughter on a few Faith Camps, organized by Kingdom Faith Ministries, who were starting a new church in Manchester. That was a good time, but then I started a relationship with a man again and fell away from that as well. So I ended up living in a ten-year abusive relationship of domestic violence.

I felt desperate and the only reason I was getting to work was that it was the only place I felt equal to anyone else. I was not put down all the time while I was there. I loved going to work because I started working in mental health and started empowering other women. When I worked with women it helped me. Although I was supporting women who may have had previous abuse, I was going home to daily current abuse. I had compulsive addictive behaviours going on.

Then I started gambling so that I didn't have to go home to be attacked abusively, physically and mentally – we nearly lost our home. I got through this with help from my mum, but I started thinking about God again and going to church. I remembered how my friend had introduced me to Ivy Church many years before, and I came back occasionally, but I thought, "I don't fit into these places. I need some help." And I left.

Life continued to be painful so I used to sneak out to church on a Sunday morning. I went to Ivy in Didsbury. My abusive partner would say, "Where are you going? I bet you're sneaking off to that church again!" It was awful never waking up to "Good morning!" but a threatening "Where do you think you're going?" Still, I would sneak off and 'get a little bit' for that day. The benefit would soon wear off, though, because I didn't understand or feel it.

Then the abuse got worse and so did my gambling. I called the Samaritans and domestic violence lines. I called the police often. Little by little my partner's partying became more important to him and eventually he left. Within a month my gambling stopped and there was a release.

Unfortunately, I had other addictions and other needs, and so I started going on online dating sites looking for guys to just fill my life. My relationship with my daughter was going sour, because she had lived through observing this ten-year abuse.

I have had seven relationships in my life. Half have been abusive, and half with alcoholics. I have had my own addictions as well. This was a disastrous environment for my daughter and she started becoming violent towards me. I screamed at Social Services to come and take her from me as I was going to work with scratches and bruises. She was only eleven but taller than me. Looking back, I think she just treated me the way I had shown her, the way I had allowed people to treat me. I have never hit my daughter because I knew I didn't like being hit myself. But she was hitting me because she had seen others do it. That's what I believe was going on. When you're walking in the world, life is like that, isn't it? It makes you want to weep.

After all that, I got into yet another violent relationship and ended up in court with a man who put a hammer to my head amongst other things. It was the pits.

I started coming back to church a little more, but I didn't know anyone there. I'd sit at the back of the cinema where the church met at that time, crying on my own, praying for friends but at the same time praying that no one would see me in that state. Then I would walk away thinking, "I haven't met anyone today." But as I was crying, I was feeling a release and things were changing. Something was different.

I went to the front for prayer one Sunday. I don't know who was leading the meeting but they invited people to come forward and they were kneeling at the front. Someone put their hand on me and prayed. They said, "You think you've had the best, but the best is yet to come." I was the type of person who felt that every time I was in a relationship, being wanted, it was the best. Even when I was being abused or hit or I was gambling. I just wanted to be part of something and be wanted, and I thought everything was OK. "Oh, I'll probably get a better boyfriend or something," I thought.

I didn't appear to be making any progress at church but it still stuck with me.

I decided to speak to Anthony but I wasn't really able to say what I wanted to. How do you say to a pastor who is male, "I think I'm addicted to men I dated, dating sites and destructible sex/violence based relationships"? I just ended up saying, "My life's a bit of a mess and stuff." He guided me to the Freedom in Christ course. I started with that. Then somebody at church invited me to a Grow Group. Things were gradually changing. I did feel different but I knew there was something more about me that needed recovery.

I heard about the Recovery Group so I have been attending that and it has been really helping. I've been coming regularly since before Easter 2014. I come every week because I get so much from knowing Jesus and I love coming to the church. I've been to other churches but I wasn't really able to 'get it'. I don't see myself as an intellectual person and if things are said in a way where it goes right over my head, I'll think, "I'm not clever enough for this." But it's not really about that, is it?

I did the Alpha course and the CAP Money course and anything that was going on at Ivy; I just threw myself into it. I went to a meal once where the Pastor's friend was speaking. I didn't know anybody and I ended up sitting with his in-laws. I just threw myself into it and said to myself, "You can't just sit at home if you want to change your life; you've got to distract yourself." I know that God can change things, but you've got to take that step and make a choice to go.

I've started to understand that things will fall on my ears and in my heart and I'm 'getting it', you know, a bit. I know there's a lot to get and some things we will never fully get.

One day they were asking people to serve at Ivy and I found myself at the Welcome Desk asking if I could join everything! Since then I feel part of the church and am getting to know more people. I feel like I'm serving God who is helping me and healing me. It has really empowered me to want to grow and get closer to Jesus. The church says they are "helping people find their way back to God" – and they really do. I feel that the seed was planted when I was nineteen; I'm forty-five now and I'm finding my way back to God.

It was also announced in church they were doing baptisms on Easter Sunday, 2015. I made the decision to make it public that I was following Jesus, that I was serious about this. I had been baptised almost eighteen years earlier but I hadn't really understood what it was about. My baptism was an amazing experience. The church was full and friends came along. I knew I was making the best decision and it was time to move on from my old life.

Several weeks ago I felt I was set free from an old relationship. I had stalked someone in my head and in my heart, and was afraid. I had planned to go to the police because I was so emotional about it and I thought that if I didn't tell someone, I would end up sitting outside his house. He had hurt me and it was not a godly relationship or even a Christian relationship; it was based on lust. It was just me trying to fill that void in myself. We used each other but he became really hurtful and abusive. I was going to go to the police to say, "Help me! I'm going to stalk someone and I'm going to end up being arrested."

However, something happened in church. They were talking about being clean. We were given an opportunity to just sit down, bow our heads and ask God what it was we needed to hand over to make us clean. What was disqualifying me from being clean? I felt God was saying, "That stuff that you wanted to hand over to the police – don't hand it to the police, hand it to me." So I handed it to God and then I pictured myself: I was white, my house was white, my hands were white as snow, even my feet were white. In the meeting, we were talking about the dirt coming off us or on us, and I felt like God was saying, "There's the white path." As I was walking, the path was staying white but dirt was falling off my feet. I felt He was saying, "If you walk with me, the dirt will not come on to you but it will fall from you."

There were three men whom I had an obsession over. They had all hurt me. I always wanted answers but you can never get answers. Now, when I saw God telling me about this white path, I saw a picture of these three men. I saw a little white seed in each of their hearts because I had opportunities to actually forgive them and tell them that I was now walking with Jesus. I said, "I am following Jesus; he loves us and forgives us and I forgive you."

Now the little white seed is between them and God, and I am out of it. I felt a release from the obsession and the sexual need. I wanted to stalk them and it has just fallen away; I am set free. Praise God! It was an amazing time; I ran out of church and wanted to dance or fly or whatever! I can't believe how it happens but it does happen; you can be set free!

I get many opportunities working in Recovery now. I think with all this pain God will turn it around and use it for his glory. This is what

Jesus has done for my life. He can do it for others too. We all need Jesus.

I applied for a job as a senior recovery worker to lead a team of support workers in supported housing. I didn't know if I was doing the right thing. On my first day the senior that was leaving asked about shifts. When I said, "I'd like Sundays and Thursdays free, please," she asked if I was a Christian. It turned out that she was as well and she prayed with me as we sat in the office. She left that job to go on a women's mission and is now working at a healing place; she still keeps in touch a year on!

I have been working in Mental Health for six-and-a-half years. I can be a shy person and never liked to work in groups or to talk to a lot of people in a group. I still struggle with praying out loud. But I know that God is helping me. Last year, in answer to prayer, I got a job leading a team of five staff. I have worked with women for five years; now I am working with men and women. Also, my dream was to get a job empowering people through recovery from mental health issues and return to employment or education to make a difference. I was given favour out of 172 applicants. Praise God for this job! I have since met my manager at a church service and discovered she is a Christian too. She prayed with me.

So the shy girl who never wanted to speak to people is in a job where I now hold team meetings, tenants' meetings and work in guiding people. We make a difference in people's lives every day through recovery work in Mental Health. These very people that I now work for were offering me accommodation twenty years ago when I was homeless and had my own social worker. Now I am assessing people for our accommodation and everything has turned around. Praise the Lord!

I believe that even during times when I wasn't walking with God, He was always there. As for the future, I'm looking forward to my job and following Jesus – God's will, not mine. I just want to serve all the time.

I have just volunteered to help with the cooking for Soul Survivor. I know this is me just wanting to relive my youth again, but I'm cooking to serve. At first they were saying they weren't sure as they had enough people, but I was praying, "Please, I want to go! I want to go! I know this will be a blessing to others, but the blessing is for me and for them." Then I got a message from Emma Gaze: "We'd love for you to help." I was so excited about that, just blessing the young people by making them a meal.

Going through Recovery was not just about *my* healing, it was also for the healing of *my family*. My daughter lived through the violence when I was in and out of hospital and self-harming so she has suffered from depression, but our relationship is building up. I also had the opportunity to say to her, "I'm sorry."

"Sorry for what, Mum?" she asked.

Through tears I said, "For the bad choices I made in life."

She consoled me. "It's okay, Mum, because I would have lived a sheltered life!"

Now, I don't know what that means, but to me, that was her way of saying, "Mum, I forgive you." So that's something for me and my daughter. It's not where it should be, but I know it's a beginning and God is working. We did have lots of good times. She tells me I did my best as a single mum. I had my family's support – I know my family loved me and cared – it's just that stuff happens in life.

My relationship with my mum is getting better too. I told my mum some pretty bad stuff about sexual abuse I had had when I was fifteen, which I didn't know she knew about. The unfortunate thing was that I didn't pray about it first; I just walked in and told her. It went a bit badly. My mum said she had problems of her own and that she already knew. She said it had been someone I knew but I said it wasn't, that she had been passed the wrong information. I had reported it to the police when I was younger but when I knew I needed examinations, I had been frightened to go through with it, so nothing had come of it. I had been sent to live with my aunt, but had my mum and dad known what would happen, it might have been different.

My aunty lived in Somerset and had her own problems. She allowed me access to alcohol. When I was fifteen I decided to run away because I was unhappy and had been grounded. I drank alcohol given to me, and I woke up abused by four or five men in a hotel room. So after thirty years, I had decided to tell my mum.

I think my mum must have felt guilty given her response to me. So I took my bag and I ran out through the door. I decided I was never going back. But by the Monday I felt fine and I gave it all back to God. I realised that with God's help, when you have dealt with this stuff, it's over, its gone forever; you don't have to keep reliving the pain. So on the same night, even though I had decided that I was never going to see my mum again, I got in touch and made amends with her. I know now that God forgives me my mistakes and sins, and I want to forgive my mum.

I noticed another thing too. It was my birthday in June and I have an old group of friends who all have birthdays in the same month. Every year they like to go out into Didsbury and drink in the pubs, and last year I went along. When you've just started walking with Jesus at the beginning, you can be pulled back by peer pressure; these women are my friends and I've known some of them a lifetime.

"Come on, Tracey, we're going out and getting drunk. Didsbury won't know what's hit us!"

"No. Actually, I'm not doing that anymore."

This year I didn't go. I haven't got a drink problem or anything, but once I start drinking I don't like who I am. I've ended up at places I didn't know.

So the next day, I was up fresh for church and had an amazing time with my daughter. I phoned her and she answered (she never usually answers the phone). We went to Dunham Massey – one of our favourite places – and had a lovely day, and the relationship has been blessed. I didn't go out drinking; I'm showing my daughter that I'm stable and consistent, and she knows I'm back with Jesus.

I felt like she's coming back to me and I thought, "That's how God must feel when His children come back to Him. I just want to give and give, and love unconditionally." That's how I felt. I was thanking God for Jesus and everything!

I don't know how she feels about it yet but a seed has been planted in her life from the beginning. She does say, "Mum, we've been through this and we've been through that but you're doing all right now." I want her to understand that it's Jesus that has made the difference and he loves her too – but I'm sure it will come.

I keep wishing I was twenty again and that I knew then what I know now. I feel younger anyway. I feel a weight has been lifted off my shoulders. I feel free. People at Ivy have been so helpful and encouraging. People have come to help do my garden. I have so many friends.

I had twenty-five years of claustrophobia. I still have trouble getting into lifts. I'd never flown before because of fear. I missed out on holidays with my parents and siblings because of fear. But with my Recovery Group I went to Ireland on a plane for the first time! I went on a retreat and spent time with people who were like-minded and had been through addictions and past hurts but were all working towards recovery using Bible verses.

I love the church family. It's been amazing. I can't believe how my life has turned around. Growing up, I spent my life drinking in and around Didsbury, and being in a psychiatric unit. I've witnessed an unknown man pull a gun out and shoot someone in front of me in this area. All this where I now attend church, where I now live in freedom, because *Jesus sets us free.*

Onwards and upwards!

GEMMA TUSON

Age:	*36*
Family:	*Married with two children*
Started at Ivy:	*2008*
Choice of beverage:	*Decaf latte*

I was brought up in a family where my mum believed in God but didn't regularly attend church and my dad was not a believer. It wasn't until I was in my early teens that my mum started to attend a church. Growing up I always had a feeling and belief that there was a God but I never had any teaching at Sunday school.

At the age of thirteen I started to sometimes go along with her and by the time I was fifteen I decided to make a commitment and got baptised. Around that time, I got involved with one of the members of the youth group; he was eighteen years old and I was probably sixteen.

At first the relationship was innocent but after a while he started to influence me in a negative way. My teenage years involved going to church but also going out to parties and clubs and all the things that these environments bring. The relationship lasted for four years, on and off, and I didn't really grow in my faith during this time.

Afterwards I went to university and that kind of lifestyle continued. I was still going to church during this time so there was a lot of guilt attached to it. But I never had a personal relationship with God. I would always pray, "Please forgive me." I felt I was forgiven, but then I would do the same things the next weekend. It was a vicious circle; I'd go to church, ask God for his forgiveness and, in a way, abuse his grace.

I did a Fashion degree at university and I knew that in order for me to get into the industry I would have to move to London. I was very hesitant about that and thought it was about time I sorted my faith out and my relationship with God. I decided that moving to London was not going to be the best thing for me.

Around that time, I went to an Assemblies of God (AOG) conference where a man called Gerald Coates came to speak. During one of the evening meetings, he got all the youth on to the stage and prayed over us.

My Fashion degree had included studies of Fashion Photography. I had gone to London for work experience at a well-known teenage fashion magazine. While I was on that stage, God downloaded the idea of producing a relevant teenage magazine that was wholesome and relevant.

So I set about doing that the minute I finished my degree. We were blessed with some free office space, and a friend and I spent three years producing the teenage magazine. We had the most amazing time. God totally blessed it. And we saw many things happen and went all over the country with it.

But we were young. I was twenty-one when it started and we weren't great with finances. Soon we got into a difficult financial situation. We had both met our fiancés through doing the magazine. Hers was from Swansea so when she got married she moved there.

A couple from church then decided they would take the magazine on, which was great because they were a lot better with the financial side of it.

At this time my dad fell really ill with cancer, while I was planning my wedding. Things all went a bit pear-shaped. He died six weeks before my wedding day. It was one of the worst times of my life and the worst time for it to happen. I really couldn't understand *why* it had happened because we had looked at so many dates to get married and had felt this would be the right date, but if it had been any of the other dates he would have been at my wedding. So my brother gave me away and delivered the father of the bride speech that he and dad had written together. I had to move out of our family home. And within six weeks my poor mum's household had gone from three to one.

I started to get really frustrated with God. I became very angry inside and kept wondering why all this had happened. I just couldn't understand it. Having been on a real high on a journey with God, I now felt annoyed with Him. I would still go through the motions of going to church but I found it very difficult to pray. I couldn't speak to Him because I was so angry and I didn't particularly want to break down and tell Him how I felt. Everybody kept telling me I was so brave, so I thought I would just continue with the brave face and keep going, and unfortunately that lasted a few years.

I had my daughter and I still wasn't really in a good place with God. I became pregnant with my son and then I decided I needed to sort things out. So I went for some Christian counselling.

Ivy Church was reading a book together called 'Crazy Love' by Francis Chan. I didn't read it with the church but it was there on my bookshelf. One day, I noticed it and I determined I *would* read it because I knew that He really loved me and needed to understand *how* much He did, because right then I didn't feel it. Why would he hurt a daughter whom He loves and take away her father before her wedding day?

I read the book, and there was a chapter about how Jesus loves you and that if the whole of existence is a film then the starring role of that film is Jesus and your part in the story is an extra. It said that if you were to go and watch the film, you probably wouldn't even see yourself because you would just be amongst the crowds for a millisecond. Then all of a sudden I had a great revelation: the way I was thinking about the situation was that it was *my* movie and *I* was the leading role of the movie and the wedding was the 'happily ever after' bit at the end. My thoughts were, "How could He do that to me? How could he ruin my ending?" But actually, it's not about me; it's about Jesus. What happened was this: when my dad became ill with cancer, he immediately gave his life to Jesus and went and got baptised. So he lived the last six months of his life as a Christian. And the testimony at his baptism was just amazing; all his work colleagues, family and friends were there. It was awesome! So, actually, that was the most important thing in that part of the movie – that my dad was saved and that he was with Jesus. God loves me and I am in a relationship with Him but He loves my dad just as much as He loves me. That was my realisation – that it was not about me. Obviously, for me it was my 'happily ever after' but it was not the main ending. Jesus coming back for his bride is the ending of the movie. I started to work through it all with a Christian counsellor who really helped me.

I started to get back on track. I went on a course called 'In Your Own Skin' which is designed to help women be who they want to be and who they were created to be and generally 'be comfortable in their own skin'. At the time I had had both my children and I wasn't really sure where I was headed – in work, ministry or anything. The course helped me see where I had come from and to look into the future. I wanted to do something that would make a difference. I had been there before and I felt that was where I wanted to be again.

I work freelance doing lots of different creative things, and part of that is working with young girls doing fashion workshops during school holidays. I had reached a place where I was considering giving up this area of my work and starting up a business.

I had been getting closer to God and I hear Him quite clearly about things. For a few months I had kept hearing that I was going to die and I didn't understand it. I asked, "God is this true? Is this right?"

"Yes."

"Where?"

"It's going to happen in your car."

" *What* is going to happen?" (It was very strange.)

That summer I went to Faith Camp with my mum's church and I heard the same thing again. I felt like it was going to happen soon and so I drove home with my children in the car thinking, "Is it going to happen? Is it going to happen?" But nothing happened. Obviously!

The very next day I was on my way to London to do some workshops with some girls and I was going to be there for a whole week. I thought, "Something's going to happen tomorrow in the car and I have just got to trust God. I have just got to absolutely trust that He knows what is going on."

I said goodbye to my family, not knowing whether it was going to be the last time I would see them.

When we were in Peterborough at Faith Camp, I had introduced my daughter to her Kids Club workers but they had got her name mixed up and incorrectly called her Emerald the whole time she was there. On one of the days I was just about to get on to the motorway when a white van pulled in front of me with the word 'Emerald' in green letters across the back of it. "Wow, God," I thought, "what was that all about?"

I decided to play some music. It was sunny and I had my sunglasses on. I stuck some worship music on and all of a sudden my car was filled with the Holy Spirit! It was just full; it was thick and I was crying, driving along and praising Jesus. Then just as we were coming to Birmingham it went completely black. It was daytime but there were many clouds and it was really stormy. I thought, "Something's going to happen now. Is this it? Is this what's going to happen?"

The heavens opened and it threw down huge hailstones. It was so bad that every car slowed down to 30mph on the motorway. I prayed, "Lord, my life is in Your hands! My life is in Your hands! My... life... is... in... Your... hands! Whatever is going to happen, my life is in Your hands!"

I just prayed and prayed. I felt like I was on top of a rollercoaster and I was speaking in tongues. "I'm giving You everything. I'm giving You everything. Everything that I am is Yours. If this is it, if I am going to die now, that is fine. I will trust You. I absolutely trust you!"

I pulled through the storm and it suddenly stopped. "What just happened?" I thought. I pulled in at a nearby service station. I was *so* shaken and spent about an hour praying. I asked Him, "What has just happened?"

He said, "You have just died to yourself. You just gave *everything* to me!"

"Oh my goodness, *I did!* I will put myself completely in Your hands. Whatever You want me to do, I am going to do it."

That week God absolutely broke my heart over the girls that I had worked with. They had shared so much about their lives and I had felt so glad that I was there for them. But now I was leaving. I was never going to see those girls again. I felt I needed to be doing something where I lived, making a difference with young girls.

I think, actually, He brought me back in line with what had been my original ministry. It was as if that was always what I should have been doing. It's just that there had been a very long pause in the middle. It's been a decade of family and heartbreak and other things.

I started getting lots of dreams. I originally thought I was going to write a book about my story but I didn't think I would have enough words to write a book. Yet I still felt there was something. I had a dream and I kept seeing, "Beloved, Beloved, Beloved." Then I kept seeing, "Be-Loved Beloved, Be-Loved Beloved, Be-Loved Beloved." I thought, "Is this the name of a book?" So I wrote it down and then started getting ideas for chapters: "Be Free", "Be You", "Be Bold", "Be Still", "Be Focussed", "Be Creative" – all these different things, and I thought, "God are these the chapters of the book?"

He said to me, "No, it's a course. I want you to write a course for young women."

So I started to write a course and it was so difficult. I'd never written anything like it before. It was a hard labour, but I wrote the course and still felt that there was a book. I asked, "Lord, what's this book?"

I had a few more words and another dream, and God said to me, "It's a journal for the girls to use during the course."

So I have designed an interactive journal that has all six sessions within it. There are no print-out sheets; it's all there in the journal.

It's taken years now and I didn't think it would take me this long, but it has been an amazing process because there is a great deal that God has been doing within me. I feel that's why it has taken time – He's been changing my heart and has given me a massive love for so many more people.

And I think, because it's called 'Be Loved' and it's all coming from a place of "You are so greatly loved", He's having to do a work on me as well.

So my journey has been very long and quite painful, but right now I am in a place where I know what God wants me to do. I have a great heart for the vulnerable ones who just don't know how amazing they can be in God. I am linking up with different charities that are working with vulnerable girls. This is where I am meant to be.

Onwards and upwards!

GILLIAN BERRISFORD

Age:	*59*
Family:	*Single*
Started at Ivy:	*1977*
Choice of beverage:	*Tea*

My early years were fine; I was brought up in a Christian home, so no problems there really. Then I rebelled at about thirteen and stopped going to church. I went to college, and at eighteen an old school friend invited me to Bethshan Tabernacle in Levenshulme. I thought it would be 'a laugh' so I went along.

I became a Christian that night!

I didn't go back to my mum and dad's church because it was a very, very exclusive Brethren church – and Bethshan wasn't. So I carried on going there until I moved to Manchester at age twenty-one. I worked for Manchester City Mission in Salford, and I started going to Ivy Church because Ray Miller, whom I knew, said how good it was. So I joined them, and on and off I have been there ever since. I have had a few breaks when I have been abroad but I have always ended up coming back to Ivy.

In my mid-twenties I read a book about Amy Carmichael, a missionary from Ireland who went out to India. I explored a bit more and felt God saying that I should go out there and see the country. I wrote to a friend of mine who lived in India and worked amongst the deaf, a mission which was started by Amy. She invited me over. So I went for six months at about the age of twenty-seven or twenty-eight. At one point we visited Dohnavur for a weekend and I felt God was calling me there for a longer time.

When I returned to England, I worked for Scripture Union in one of their bookshops in Stockport and at the same time I explored returning to India. The first time I applied to go I was turned down, because you have to go for life and sign up for life and they felt my parents weren't behind me. I continued at Scripture Union but after three years I still felt God was calling me to India. I reapplied and this time they said, "Yes, we've prayed about it and we think you are right; can you come?"

So in March 1984, I went to live in Dohnavor. It should have been for life, but after three and a half years the British Government changed their visa regulations. I had gone on a Commonwealth visa and suddenly India's law stated it was not possible to remain on that visa. You had to have either a Business Visa or a Missionary Visa, which I could not get because they were trying to get rid of missionaries. So in 1987, I came back home.

I had a rough year because I was very confused as to why God had called me out there only to have me come back again. Fortunately, there was a job opening again at Scripture Union. I said to God, "I gave my flat up and I gave my job up when I went to India. You can call me anywhere you want." Surprisingly, He called me right back to Manchester, back to Ivy and back to the job I had left, which was very odd!

I worked there for another year, when I met Dennis and Jane. I had known Dennis for many years through Ivy and we all lived together in a big house in West Didsbury called Charter House, which was half ex-convicts from Strangeways Prison and half Christians from Ivy! Dennis had got married while I was in India and his wife was expecting twins. So I just felt it was right to offer my services to them and they took me on as their nanny for their daughters, who are now twenty-six!

I worked for them for the next four years. Then they felt God calling them to Thailand and asked me to come with them. By that time, they had another daughter as well, so when the twins were four and a half and their youngest was eighteen months, we all went to Thailand. I felt it was not right for them to go and not have anyone to help them look after the children; so I volunteered to go with them. They had to study for seven months in language school and I looked after the children while they were there.

Then I returned yet again and had various jobs, first back at Scripture Union and nannying for families at Ivy after working in a nursery for a very short time.

I didn't really like the nursery because I was used to having a one-to-one with a child. Then Anne and Colin, who are now abroad, were having their first baby and asked me to look after their daughter, so I helped them. Since then I have helped so many families at Ivy, I have lost track!

I had my final 'baby' from eight weeks until he was five years old and then he went to school. By then my health had deteriorated badly; I had had surgery in 2000 to have a valve replacement and then I went back to work. I was looking after a little girl for three or four years but my situation deteriorated further and I needed a pacemaker in 2007. I had to really start praying if it was right to still look after children. I took on this last child, but by the time he went to school I was quite ill and everybody decided that looking after children was no longer feasible as I had quite bad heart failure at the time.

I had a year off work recovering from that, and at the same time I was looking after my mum, which I realise now was part of God's plan. I was travelling up to Buxton alternate weekends to do all her cooking and cleaning until I got quite ill. Then she had to go in a home, following which she died in June 2012.

While all this was happening, I was signed off work so it worked out well in moving her into a nursing home and clearing her house. They only gave you twelve months on Employment Support Allowance and when my year came to an end I wondered what I was going to do next.

However, I had done some computer training while I was off ill, through the Job Centre. A friend from church rang me to say there was a job coming up at Dignity (a Christian charity working into Africa) and, would I be interested, because I had happened to have a chat with him at a missionary event that had taken place at Ivy.

He said, "So what are you doing at the moment?"

I replied, "Well, nothing, but I am looking for an office job because I am training in computer skills."

We went through the due process of C.V.s and interviews, and the day after my benefit finished he rang me and said I had got the job.

I had said to him that there were three things on my tick list:

"I don't have transport so it would have to be local."

"We are at Emmanuel."

"That's fine. It has to be flexible, because I have so many hospital appointments."

"Well you can do whatever days you like."

"OK. But I can't really work full-time."

"No, we only want you sixteen hours."

"Perfect." It had ticked every box on my tick list. How amazing!

At the time I had moved from my flat in West Didsbury into a retirement block right opposite Ivy, so I just roll across the road in the evenings and it's a five-minute walk to work. My hours are flexible.

So I have been officially employed by them since January 2014 but already started working in 2013 on a self-employed basis, to see if I could do the job, before they took me on.

I have been a long time at Ivy and have seen it change hugely over the years. Sometimes I wondered whether I should stay or not. But I have always felt that unless there is a reason to leave, it is where God wants me. At the moment, because of my health, I don't think I can go abroad and get involved with mission that way, but I can get involved in supporting things by praying. It is a new season for me and I think, "Come on, Lord! Either you heal me so I can do more, or you show me what I can do within my limitations."

When I was ill, I went into the Ivy office and said, "Is there anyone who needs my help, because I could type or I can do admin?" So Dave asked around if people thought I could do it. They all said, "Of course she can!"

I had never used an iPad before I started at Ivy, but I love it and I have my own now. It has opened up completely new horizons for me.

I come to all the Dignity meetings and I think, "Well I can't go to Zambia, even if I wanted to, because of the costs of the health insurance, which would be more than the flight, but I know that I can stay in the office and support the missions team from there while they fly out."

Onwards and upwards!

CALLY

Age: *48*
Family: *Married with three children*
Started at Ivy: *2008*
Choice of beverage: *Fruit juice*

I grew up in a loving Christian home with my parents, older sister and younger brother. Although my parents didn't go to church until I was ten, I always knew that they believed and they passed that on to me. We did occasionally go to church at Christmas.

I moved to Paris because of my dad's job and lived there for three years. It was there that we started to go to an English church and I also found out about a Bible study in someone's home that some of the children from my English school attended after studies. I used to pray to God by myself a lot and knew that God was real and answered prayers. However, I was very shy and found it hard to talk in a group.

When I was eleven, I went to a Bible study. Each week the teacher would ask if anyone would like to pray and everyone stayed silent. I remember feeling the fear when one day the Bible teacher asked again and I surprised myself by saying I would pray. I prayed a simple prayer for God's blessing and help for us all to know him better. I believe God gave me the courage that day, and from then on the other children also gained the courage to pray at the end of the lesson. I felt glad to have been an inspiration to them.

During that summer, I went to a camp for just three days at a Bible school in Paris, which some of the leaders and some of the students there organised for the children. I learnt there that when you believe you need to confess it and tell somebody that you have actually made that commitment to God. I knew I believed but it felt scary to tell others about my faith. I prayed for God's help and he again gave me courage; I stepped forward to pray to accept Jesus into my heart and then I told my parents and my best friend that this had happened to me. I was so happy because I was now born again, a new creation – a child of God. This was where my journey with God really began.

Then we moved back to Britain because of my dad's job and we all started going to the local Presbyterian church. I decided to be confirmed there and in the confirmation lessons I asked the minister about the Holy Spirit. However, I felt I wasn't receiving a complete answer from him and I was curious to learn more.

At the age of fifteen I hurt my leg in an accident at school while I was playing squash. I had my leg operated on and put in a cast. A couple who moved in across the road with two young children said they were starting a church up at their house and asked if I wanted to come along, because I couldn't make it to my own church. I agreed and joined them.

It was just that family and me to start with and I loved it. I genuinely felt like a part of their family and I learnt that miracles happen today. I grew up staying in that church and the church grew in that house. It was there that I learnt about the power of the Spirit, that we need to pray and ask for the gift of tongues and pray for the sick. I learnt that God had given me the gift of tongues.

From the church across the road from me I learnt that the Holy Spirit is real and a person, that He is part of the Holy Trinity, that He is always with us and that He never leaves us nor forsakes us. It was a big step forward to learn all that about God. I also learnt that there is a battle going on and we have the Holy Spirit with us to give us confidence; He is the one who wins all of the battles.

I was still young and went through many difficulties in my life. I had Myalgic Encephalomyelitis (ME) from the age of fourteen till I was twenty-eight, so I was struggling health-wise. But God gave me the courage to keep going and to keep hoping for things.

Also when something happened to me and I got suicidal thoughts, it was God who got me through it. Once I was in my room and a man came in through the window, someone I knew to say hello to but did not know well. I just froze in fear and he touched me inappropriately, but I managed to stop him doing anything further. Although nothing much happened, I felt angry with myself because I hadn't managed to stop this man quicker. I felt so dirty and so terrible that I had suicidal thoughts after that. I didn't tell anyone though. When I went through it, I felt like there was no hope at all; there was just utter despair and I felt things would never get better. I didn't try to commit suicide and I didn't think of a plan, but the thoughts were very strong. And when I came through it, I remember acknowledging that it was a total lie from the devil; there *was* hope, things *did* get better!

It was a horrible experience. But before it happened a lady from my church had had a dream or a vision of me. She saw me wrapped around by a horrible snake, but finally it fell off. She didn't know what it represented but it really, really scared her. It was as though the devil was attacking me. The whole church prayed for me and also said that when I got through whatever it was, I was to help others.

Although I didn't tell anyone about the suicidal thoughts at that time, my kind mother realised I was depressed and went to the doctor with me. There I was prescribed antidepressants. In later times, when I had suicidal thoughts again, I had the strength to say, "This is just a lie," even though it didn't feel like it; I knew that God was with me and the devil was lying to me.

When I was at university I wasn't really going to church, but I did know that God was with me. However, there was a time later, after I moved to another city, that something happened again in which I froze and felt terrible. I managed to stop anything serious from happening, but I just felt awful again. I was trying to get back into fellowship and church and now this had happened.

I remember hanging my head and feeling awful, thinking God wouldn't accept me now, when I heard a sound like knocking. It just kept going on. I started to wonder if it was real or whether it was in my head, and still it continued. It was almost as if someone was knocking next door, yet I could hear the knocking in my head and it was rhythmic. "What is that, God?" I thought. Then I saw a picture with a hand and a nail being hammered into it. It was as if God was saying, "I have paid for it all." Yes, He *has* paid for it all. It was the realisation that Jesus has paid for all our sins. *Everything* is paid for. We can start anew with God, who forgives us just like that.

I came back to church and was able to go back with confidence after university. I had met an African woman who went to an art class with me and hoped to get this woman's details on the last day, as I wanted to go to the fellowship that she had told me about, but she didn't come. So I prayed that I would meet her. Then I happened to see her on the bus so I asked if I could get her number quickly before either of us had to get off.

Later I called her up and started to attend the Christian fellowship. I felt totally at home there. I was really happy to be in the fellowship and I went to the church that was connected to it as well.

People had been telling me about a man called Sean, who was away in London. They said he had started a church, although only children had come initially, and when he returned I would probably meet him. I said, "Oh I'd like to help in the Sunday school, because I love children." So when he arrived, I was introduced to him and I said that I would love to come along. Although I wasn't sure if it would be right for me, I would try it out.

In my mind I remembered Sunday schools from my younger years, in which everyone was so well-behaved. So I thought, if it was anything like that, would I be of any use at all?

On the first day I went there, they were having a trip to the park. There were about twelve or so children and maybe three leaders. So I went along and everything seemed to be fine, although you knew from the children that things were going on because if you tried to get them off the swing they would say, "Don't touch me or else I will tell my social worker." You knew from this kind of attitude that they lived their life on the street and just went home to their parents at night; they were always out and were quite tough.

At the end of the trip, when we were getting everyone on to the minibus, we couldn't find one of the boys. He was only seven and he had gone missing in this big park with different sections. Sean told everyone to get on the bus and go back while he would stay and look for the boy, but I said, "No, I will stay with you, and we can pray and look for this boy together." So the other adult with us took the children home on the minibus.

We walked around everywhere, looking under the bushes, calling him and couldn't find him – but we kept praying. Then we reached a car park. I thought, "Well, he's not going to be in a car park, because children don't want to play in a car park!" But I heard a voice in the back of my mind telling me to wait there; he would be there in a minute. I thought, "Well, that's not me because I wasn't thinking that. I was thinking of carrying on looking in the park." So I told Sean. He looked puzzled but agreed.

A minute later a policeman pulled into the car park with the little boy in the back seat. He got out and the policeman said to the boy, "You see. I told you they wouldn't have driven off and left you." We had such amazing joy at seeing him. He'd actually had the sense to go into a phone box and dial 999 and call the police. So we just thanked God for his wisdom and that He had spoken to me as well and said, "Just wait." God helps us when we are lost and helps us to be found again. He helps us in our deepest needs.

This was my first real day at this Sunday school, and I realised I was really needed. My relationship with Sean grew at that time. Sean is a great Bible teacher; I learnt so much from him. Gradually, the Sunday school became a little church and he became the minister. I became the Sunday school teacher and so we spent a good time there.

Sean and I became close, and he realised that he needed to pray for healing for me. He did pray – and I was healed from M.E. After fourteen years of having that illness I was finally free from the aching muscles and the fatigue I had suffered.

One day, I went to see a family to tell them about the Sunday school I was running. They were a couple with two young children whom I had lived opposite previously; it was in quite a deprived area. I had thought that it might be a good idea for these children to go to the Sunday school and I had spoken to the woman before but the man had been very reclusive. He was in fact an alcoholic.

I decided to speak to the mother. I went there and buzzed up from downstairs because they lived on the first floor, and I asked if she was there. The husband said, "Oh yes, come on up." So I did, thinking she would be there, and he let me in. He showed me through to the sitting room and said, "Actually, she's not here."

"Oh!" I exclaimed.

"But she'll be here in a few minutes."

I wondered, should I wait or go? I decided to wait for a few minutes.

The husband showed me some pictures and we were having a normal conversation, when I announced that I needed to go because I was going to meet someone.

His reply was, "I will go with you in your car."

"No," I insisted, "I need to go alone."

Then he suddenly switched. He blocked the door and said, "You are not leaving; you have to stay here."

I was there for four hours. Everything just escalated. He was really rough, pushing me back and saying that I could not leave.

I said, "Look, if you hurt me, if you do anything to me, you're going to prison, because you know I would have to tell the police. Think about your wife. If you do anything to me, what would she say?"

I had been talking to him about God before that and so I had this strong, clear manner of speaking to him. He kept switching between being this angry, aggressive person and a normal-sounding person. So it was God's help and encouragement that got me through that; normally, I am a quiet person who doesn't stand up to anyone. Normally, I would just freeze, like in the past.

He took me through to the kitchen and I thought he wanted a cigarette as he put on the gas ring. I thought I was in danger of being burnt there. Then he picked up a kitchen knife and I thought, "Oh, my God, I don't know what's going to happen here." In my heart I cried out to the Lord.

The man pushed me on to a kind of couch. He suggested that we could make love.

I said, "No, because I don't agree, and you know that it takes two to agree to that." I had to act as if I was his mother and have the authority even though he was strong and had a weapon. I had to be really courageous and say it several times. Then he sat up and got off me.

It came to a point when he thought he wanted to go and buy alcohol. He wanted to borrow money off me and finally I gave him £5 which I had in my purse. He planned to go to the shop. Then he thought I would run away. I said I would just stay and wait but he was not convinced, so he decided that at knifepoint he would tie me up.

He jabbed his knife into my throat and I could feel its sharp tip. He tied my arms at the back with some cables and then he had some brown masking tape to put over my mouth. I spoke as calmly as I could, "Look, I don't breathe well through my nose. If you put that over my mouth, you might kill me." He said he didn't care. He said he was from Ireland and the Irish know how to hurt people. I kicked the tape under the table, but he found it, taped my mouth, pushed me on to the bed and then tied my legs.

From the cupboard he took something out and said, "This is a bomb. If you open this door it will go off." And then he left.

I looked out of the window and I remember thinking that this could be the last thing I would ever see, because I didn't know if I was going to live anymore. I couldn't speak; I couldn't even pray. I couldn't think of words to pray so I started praying in tongues. Then, as I looked at the door, I could see that it was not a bomb; it was a firework. I managed to wriggle free a bit and hopped over to the door, gathered courage and opened it. I couldn't be completely sure if it was a bomb or not but I guessed it was a firework.

I hopped to the door that was on the landing on the first floor and I opened that, then I hopped across to knock on the door of my old flat but there was nobody home. I thought, "That shop was not far from here; he'll be back any minute. I don't think I should go down, because he might see me on the way out." So I decided to go to the floor above and as the chord had loosened between my arms and feet, I was able to hop up, and the tape was loosening a bit on my mouth from saliva.

I had got to about the sixth step when he returned. Here I was trying to escape and I knew he would be angry. So I hopped down a few steps, because he would otherwise pull me down and I needed to be safe.

He pulled my hair down on to the concrete floor from about three steps up. I smashed on to the ground. Then he grabbed it again and pulled me from my hair back into his flat.

This is when I decided to scream.

I screamed as loud as I could. He put his hand over my mouth but I just bit him. It was instinctive. Then he grabbed me and pulled me into the hallway of his flat and closed the door.

I looked up at him and simply said, "How dare you treat me like that! Untie me now!"

He looked at me and didn't seem to understand at first.

I shouted again, "Untie me now! You can't treat me like this. You can't treat anybody like that!"

And he just switched back to normal at that point. He untied my hands and then went to wash his hands.

When he came back I said, "Untie my feet and get me a glass of water. Look, I'm bleeding. My mouth is bleeding. Get me a glass of water!" And he went and got me a glass of water. (It was actually *his* blood as I'd bitten his hand hard!)

By the time he returned I had stood up. He said, "Sorry, sorry for what's happened." I tried to get my purse together and my head together.

I went to the sitting room. He opened the big windows and he said, "Just scream now, if you want to. Just scream."

I looked out of the window and realized that if I screamed out of it and he switched personality again, he could just push me down on to the spiked railings below.

So I said, "No, it's okay."

Soon after, I heard somebody at the door and I rushed to it. It was his wife returning.

I said, "Hi, I'm going!"

"What's happened here?" she asked. "What's happened here?"

I rushed down to the car and she rushed after me.

"I just have to go," I gasped.

She looked right at me and said, "He's just lost his grandmother, and it's affected him, you know."

I said, "Look, I just have to leave now."

I drove off quickly. I can still recall every traffic light; when I stopped, I just started screaming, until I carried on driving and got home. I called family and friends and told them about what had happened. My mum rushed over from another city to comfort me and said, "You'll need to tell the police because if he does it to someone again, what if he kills them?"

I said, "You're right, I do need to tell the police about it."

He went to court and he got three years in prison. In the meantime, I have forgiven him because he appeared from his changing personality to have mental health problems. So I honestly *have* forgiven him and it was God's grace that helped me in that.

I went for Christian counselling, years later, with the lady who ran the church I previously attended. She talked me through everything that had happened and told me that Jesus was with me through every step of the way. God gave me courage and wisdom to get through it all.

Looking back over this time in my life, I realise that God was with me through the good and bad times, helping me to grow stronger to be able to overcome the difficult things I had to face. God has healed the hurts and memories from the frightening events from the past. He has delivered me from the fear that I had. He has helped me to forgive myself as well as others.

I have been through a lot of difficult times and felt strongly that I should help others, which is why I went into counselling, so that I could be a help to other people. After finishing the counselling aspect of my course, I am now working as a Christian Counsellor. I am going to research more into the area of sexual abuse and shame so that I will be better able to help others who may have had similar experiences to mine.

I married Sean two years after we met. We have been married for twenty years now and we still have a great love for each other. We honour and respect each other and our marriage vows. We have three lovely children, each a unique and wonderful gift from God. I give God all the glory for helping me and saving me, and for how he helped me through so many difficult times.

For anyone who will read my testimony, I want you to know that you have a Father in heaven who loves you so much and that His love can never be shaken. If you have been abused or you feel you've messed up along the way, He longs for you to come to Him. He loves you with an everlasting love and is a forgiving God and so merciful. He will bind up your broken heart and restore your soul. He delights in you and says you are very, very precious to Him and that He has great plans for your future.

Onwards and upwards!

BABS BRAY

Age: *56*
Family: *Married with two children*
Started at Ivy: *2012*
Choice of beverage: *Americano*

I have been married to my husband for five years. We came to Ivy Church because my son from my previous marriage was a member. We are very happy here.

Before that I had been happily married for twenty-six years to my first husband, whom I met when we were really young, still teenagers at the church which we both used to go to. We grew up together and got married when we were both twenty-one. We had two children and everything was going fine, working within the church. We were both in a band and led worship. We did lots of things together and lots with the children, all revolving around the church. We then went to another church because we had a few issues where we were.

My husband got involved with the youth club and he started to co-lead the group, but unfortunately he started having an affair with another leader. She was ten years younger than him and, to make it worse, she was also my friend. She was someone whom I would go and have coffee with and went around Stockport with.

It went on for about nine months, and I didn't know anything about it. So you can imagine that it was quite a shock when I found out through text messages. The night I made the discovery I thought, "I don't know what to do!" My son was eighteen at the time and he just sat watching telly, joking about it and saying it was probably just one of the kids from the youth club who had taken the lady's phone and played a trick. So we just joked together about it – but then I found further evidence and realized, "*No...* this is not a joke, this is *real.*"

All I could do was pray because I didn't know whether to cry or to be angry. I didn't know who to phone; I didn't know what to *do*. I just prayed and said, "Lord, *you* need to do something, because I don't even know how to pray or how to respond!"

Looking back, I am so glad that praying was the first thing that I did because I could have gone out and bought a gun. That is how I felt! I wanted to go out and shoot them both.

While the affair had been going on, it had devastated quite a lot of people, especially children in the youth club. It had a ripple effect all through the congregation; the church was completely devastated and turned upside down because of all this.

Even through that time I really knew I had to handle things properly. My mum was suffering with cancer and was in hospital, so I was visiting her more or less every day, as well as working. But I just knew I had to handle everything in the right way and I had to go through forgiveness.

My husband promised to pay the mortgage. I was relieved because I looked at my bank balance and thought, "God, I can't do this. I can't financially live in this house; it's just not doable." I tweaked my outgoings and cut back where I could. And then, three months down the line, I got a letter from the building society saying that I was in arrears with my mortgage. I realised then that he had not been paying the debt.

While all this was happening, I received many text messages from him saying, "You're not having this," and, "You're not having that." I was bombarded with lies so I knew I just had to keep giving it all to God and not retaliate. I *felt* like retaliating but I knew that I had to deal with it all in the right way.

"God, I can't cope financially; I need you to intervene," I prayed. For the next six months God completely provided for me. In the first month I trusted Him for £10 – and I got the £10. The next month I thought, "Oh great, God sent me £10 last month, so I'm going to trust Him for more." So each month I just trusted Him and people put money into my bank account. "Wow!" I thought. "They don't even know my problems, and yet they're putting money into my bank account."

I had so much wrong with the house at that time. Just to give you one example, I had a problem with my gas fire. The gas man came and said, "I can't do anything with it; you need a new fire."

"I can't afford a new fire," I protested.

"Oh," he replied, "they're only £100 from B&Q."

But I explained, "I haven't got £100."

So he said, "Well, look, I can't do anything. You either go cold or you go to B&Q and spend £100."

I realised I would have to go to the shop. We didn't have any central heating in my house; the fireplace was my only source of heat. So I went to B&Q and gave them my debit card. "God," I prayed, "you know I haven't got this money. You know I'm spending this £100 because I have to."

The very next day, a Saturday, someone came up to me in church and said, "I really had you on my mind yesterday."

"What is she going to say?" I wondered.

"I really feel to give you this cheque," she continued. "I don't know why."

"Oh, right..." I mumbled.

I looked at the cheque – £100. "Wow!" I exclaimed. "You don't know what I was doing yesterday in B&Q!"

"Oh, well, I couldn't get you off my mind," she explained.

I told the whole story to her. She was very encouraged and so was I.

That's only one of many examples of how God provided for me. I really believe that if you do things in the right way, and you do everything as Jesus would do, God will bless you. I think that through those experiences my son came closer to God because he was living with me and saw all of the miracles.

Somebody came to me and asked if I wanted a lodger. They said that the NHS were paying. So I said, "Yep, whatever!" That was provision and another month's mortgage paid.

Then I said, "Right, Lord, you know what I need now: another lodger."

My son said, "Someone is looking for a place for a few weeks."

I said, "Yep! Great, bring it on!" So he came and ended up staying a year! And I thought, "Wow! That just paid my mortgage fees."

However, on the sixth month of my mortgage, I had a shortage of finances and considered moving house. The mortgage was over £300 and I didn't have the money, but I chose to just trust God. The money was due on the sixth day of the month and as the day came closer, I started to panic a little; I needed the money but it had not come. And I found myself praying a bit harder: "Lord, you know I need this money by the sixth!"

The fourth day arrived, then the fifth, and I thought, "Aww, what is this?" I'd heard many stories of people who had written the cheques to make payments, even without money in the bank, but they had just gone and given the cheque. Maybe I needed to do that. Maybe God was saying to me, "Test of faith. Do it!"

So I made my decision. I got my cheque book... but then I thought, "No, I'll just ring the building society."

So I called them and said, "Look, my mortgage is due on the sixth."

"What do you mean?" the girl asked.

"Well, if I don't pay it on the sixth I'm going to be... you know, I'll be..."

"Oh, no, no, just wait a minute," she said and she put me on hold. A few minutes later she returned. "No, you won't be in arrears for another three weeks, and by that time the sale of your home will have gone through. So you won't need to pay that money!'

Wow! That was why God didn't send it – because I didn't even need it for that month! So that's another example of God's provision.

The divorce went through. I moved into a flat and my son continued living with me because he wasn't yet married.

My ex and I had a little account on a house together, which we rented out. So we had a small bank account; there wasn't much in it, about £200. I told him I trusted him to give me half, which was about £100, and he agreed to arrange it. However, after several months I heard nothing. I texted him a few times, but received no reply and then I got a text saying there was no more money.

I thought, "He owes me £100!" I was really, really angry and wanted to go round to his home and accuse him of stealing the £100 from me. I was ranting and raving about it, when it dawned on me that I first needed to pray about it. So I said, "Lord, my source isn't him; my source is You! Why am I going on about this £100? If You want to send me £100, You can do it." So I dropped it.

The very next day I got £100 through my door. I couldn't believe it! I thought, "It's not from my ex, because if it was, he'd have made me aware." So I began to share this story wherever I went: "Guess what happened? I got £100 through my door!"

Then a few weeks later, after I had told this story many times, my friend said to me, "I need to tell you something!"

"What's that?" I asked.

"That £100 was from me."

I gulped. "Oh, right!"

She said, "I don't know anything about this bank account, but one evening I said to my husband, 'We need to go round and see Babs and give her £100.' He agreed but was worried about the timing. 'We can't go now because it's too dark. It's late. Can't we go another time?' But I insisted, 'We need to go *now*.' So we put our coats on, stuck the money in an envelope and we actually waited around the corner until we knew you had gone to bed and the curtains were closed; then we stuck the money through the letterbox."

I was flabbergasted. She was obedient to what God was telling her. It was proof to me that God is my source and that no matter what anybody does to you, it doesn't really matter, because all your provision is from Him, not from anybody else.

So I started getting really positive about all this. I started listening to Joyce Meyer's teaching at that time. I couldn't get enough of her; I couldn't get enough of the Bible. That was my best time of my whole life probably, looking back on it, because that's when I learned so many things. I was up every week testifying to what God had shown me during the week, or to a miracle, or something else.

I said to myself, "Do you know what? You're not even fifty yet; you need to get a life. I believe there is somebody out there for you. Why should you sit back and pretend your life is over? Your life is not over!"

I went on the Internet and found a Christian dating site where I met quite a few men who were all very nice. I had coffees and meals out with them. They were nice Christian chaps, but that was all it was, really; there was nothing romantic in it. I prayed about each one.

There was another man whom I really got on with. I was due to meet him in Birmingham. He agreed to come up from Southampton to meet halfway. We both booked the day off work on a day in November. Then I thought, "I really need to pray about this." Even though we really liked each other, I needed to pray because we were making a big effort.

The very next day I got an email from him saying he had met a lady at his church. He still wanted to meet up but he said he'd had a coffee with her and they were really getting on well. He wanted to be honest but still wanted to meet me. I was really 'gutted' when I read that email. Then I thought, "Wait a minute. I've prayed about this! I should be jumping off the chair! This is God telling me it is not right."

So I emailed him back and wrote, "Look, I have prayed about this, actually, and maybe it isn't right. I'm happy to still email you and chat." He just emailed back, "Okay then, that's fine." And so God put a stop to it, because I could have gone along with it in a moment of romance.

I joked to my friend, "Do you know what? I could meet somebody before the date that I was supposed to meet him on."

She laughed, "Babs, you've got loads of faith."

Believe it or not, I actually did meet someone. His name was Paul. When I started talking to him, I thought, "Yeah, this one I really get!" We got on really well and, to cut a long story short, we ended up getting married and then coming to Ivy, because we wanted to come to a church together.

At that time, I had to go through a healing process. I've had to go through forgiveness for the hurt, the anger and the rejection I previously experienced. It felt worse than death, because you never get answers, you never get an apology. I wrote to my ex and told him I wanted to thank him for everything he had done. I told him he had been a good father. I just wanted to clear everything and do everything that I thought was right between me and God. I never got a reply but it didn't matter.

I just know that as long as we keep doing the right thing, it doesn't matter about anybody else. I am happily married now. I have grandchildren and I can just say that that was the most important time that I went through in my life because I saw so much in that time.

Now I just want to help people because I have a burden for hurting women. I think I know how they feel when they have had a husband who has had an affair. But through it all I know that God was there and I did the right thing, and that's fine. I've got a heart for women who are hurting. I have spoken at a few women's meetings, sharing my story. What I discover in those meetings is a lot of unforgiveness. I went on a holiday for single women and there were many who were very angry.

"My husband had an affair."

"I don't trust men."

"They're all the same."

"Why me, why did it happen to me?"

"Why not the woman next door, who isn't even a Christian?"

I realized there must be many women out there who don't know how to get over that unforgiveness and how to cope after an affair. So since this has happened I've always had that feeling that I want to help other women who can't get over it. I've asked God to open doors in his time.

Onwards and upwards!

TRICIA RAMAROZAFY

Age:	*38*
Family:	*Recently married!*
Started at Ivy:	*2009*
Choice of beverage:	*Americano with hazelnut syrup*

I was born into a Christian family, one of six siblings. We grew up in a Pentecostal church. Church is all I've ever known. We went to different services every day, but at that age it was more of a family ritual and a cultural expectation.

So as a teenager exploring faith, exploring life, there was a bit of a journey to be made. As a student I went away from church, but not necessarily away from God. During those years, I stepped away from what I had grown up with, exploring church and visiting different churches but not really committed.

My serious faith life started in my early twenties, when it became more real and it became my decision that "this is what I want to do". There was nobody making me do it anymore. There was nobody watching. I wasn't living at home. There was no kind of family expectation.

When I was about twenty-three, I moved to America, just for work experience, and again that was me searching. At that time, I found myself talking to God. I was not really anchored in a church but found myself declaring, "God, I know you are there, I need you," and things like that. I felt that during the year-and-a-half I was away, my relationship with God grew quite strong. It was there I began to identify and recognise his voice and his presence on a daily basis.

At this crucial time, I was diagnosed with Rheumatoid Arthritis. I started getting symptoms. I was stiff with swollen joints and suffering extreme pain but it was a really weird period, because it was also when I felt I was especially close to God. It was a time of questioning Him and my faith.

At this time my confidence was shattered as this disease began to affect my mobility and daily self-care. The fact that it was affecting my whole life challenged my identity. It began to influence my thinking about who I was, my faith and what that meant in terms of Christ's love for me.

"Does He love me?"

"What does that mean?"

"The Bible says that there is healing. What does that mean? How does that work?"

So it was quite a challenging time, but God put something in me that was quite strong: a passion that God could do it. I would say to myself, "Yeah, okay, I'm in pain, but *God can do it.* Yeah, I know the doctors are saying this, but *God can do it!"*

I came back to England in 2000 and started going to church. Sometimes as the worship leader I would be in so much pain whilst leading, but I just thought, "God you're going to do it, you're going to do it. There's a miracle here and you're going to do it!" Sometimes God does things in really strange ways because in the midst of your storm, that's where He's really close, and it is about being able to listen and to hear His voice and to feel His peace in those kinds of stormy moments.

There were lots of things I had to battle with during that time, like self-esteem, whether I was worthy of having a partner etc. Who would want to marry someone who had a disability? How was that going to affect my life? Could I even work? So many different highs and lows... but as a singer, as someone who liked to worship and as a worship leader, I found a space in God's presence, a secure place in worship. Sometimes I would be in pain at home and I would just start to worship God, and He would descend on me. Once I felt like He was giving me a hug; it is hard to explain, but it was as though He was assuring me that He was with me and that He had me safe.

Psalm 91 is a scripture that He put on my heart. I was trying to find some dedicated time to read the Bible on a daily basis. I think Ivy was doing a teaching session on 'love' at the time, so I was trying to read the Bible regularly. You know how it is; we can flip through this scripture today and flip through another scripture the next day, but God gave me Psalm 91 and literally made me read it for a month... *two* months! He was affirming that I was in a safe place.

Psalm 91:1-4 says:

Whoever dwells in the shelter of the Most High will rest in the shadow of the Almighty. I will say of the Lord, "He is my refuge and my fortress, my God, in whom I trust." Surely he will save you from the fowler's snare ... He will cover you with his feathers, and under his wings you will find refuge...

I read that scripture every day, and God prompted me to read it in The Message translation. As I did, it felt like a slap on my face. Then He prompted me to read it in the NIV. It had the same effect. This was God! Sometimes we know the truth, but the truth is not connected to the heart. We go to church and hear the truth, and we know it's the truth because we have faith. But sometimes we don't actually absorb it because there is no connection there. Now God was saying, "I know you believe it, but I want you to know it in the sense that 'you know that you know that you know'."

The scripture was reaffirming as I spoke it out. It was like He was making me reaffirm His truth over myself about who He is: that He loves me, that He's my refuge, that He's my strength and that it doesn't matter what's happening, He's got me. Daddy's got me and He's not going to let me go. Daddy's not going to let anything happen to me and He's ordained certain things.

It was that reaffirmation, and what it has taught me is that no matter what we go through in life, Daddy hasn't gone anywhere; He's there. Sometimes we turn our backs on Him because we don't understand; we get angry. I've been through all those stages. I'm not going to say that it was an easy transition. There were stages that were almost like grieving because I didn't know what was happening. I didn't know what to say. I was just sad, depressed – angry, actually – because I was crying out for God.

One question I kept asking was, "Why is there no power in your Word?" We are taught that what you speak out is powerful; it's creative; there's power in the word. When you speak, things happen. So I would say, "I'm healed." Then I would wonder, "Why is nothing happening? God, why is nothing happening?" I know I don't always have the answers and we don't always understand fully what God's plans and agendas are. We always look back in hindsight and see what God saved and protected us from. We see what God is still doing in our lives and why He has to position us *here* so that we can do *that*. I can look at my whole journey and think, "Oh, God! So that's what you were doing!" It is about trust; we have to learn to trust God. That is the most important thing because in our lives we experience distrust and we experience situations which cause us to mistrust, but God's called us to trust Him because He's Daddy.

The journey hasn't ended. God has answered so many prayers but there are many more pending. I prayed for a long time about meeting the right person, getting married, and that's been a prayer for a very, *very* long time – ten years or more. However, God is faithful and I am amazed at how he answered that prayer this year.

I had discussions with people, saying, 'It's never going to happen." I saw all my friends getting married in their mid-twenties or late twenties, and by my mid-thirties I thought, "Okay, God, this is never going to happen. I just have to accept that it's not your will for me." I felt really annoyed that I hadn't met anybody and that I was still single. I felt like I was wasting my life waiting on Mr. Right. I told God, "This is not good enough! I'm sat here waiting around. What am I going to do? Maybe it's a transitional time. Maybe it's time that I go somewhere. Maybe it's time that I left the country. Maybe it's time that I did some mission work…"

So I looked for a retreat online and saw a deal in the Lake District. I thought, "Yeah, I'm going to go there, take my journal and seek God about what I'm going to do next." And that is where I met my husband – *at the retreat centre!* God is just amazing!

We think that He has forgotten and all the time He's putting the pieces together. We think, based on what we visibly see on a daily basis, that God has forgotten us and that it is never going to happen. Yet all He's doing is making sure that all the pieces are aligned correctly.

In hindsight I look back and see why everything happened the way it did. Things that were a disappointment at the time were for a purpose. Now I am happily married but it was God's divine meeting and another time when He said to me, "Tricia, are you going to trust me now? We've been on this journey for a while." I believe I am making progress in trusting God more now. It has taken some time but as I face barriers I am learning to say, "I'm not going to worry about that."

Phillippians 4:6-7 says:

> *Do not be anxious about anything, but in every situation,*
> *by prayer and petition, with thanksgiving, present your*

requests to God. And the peace of God, which transcends all understanding, will guard your hearts and your minds in Christ Jesus.

My health is still an issue; God has not healed me completely. He has healed some areas but He has not completely taken the sickness away and today I face new challenges. Newly married and getting excited about the prospects of a family, I have consultants questioning my ability to have children. But I know the God whom I serve; I know where He has taken me from up until now. I know the journey I have been through. I know exactly the points on that journey where He showed Himself strong, where He did miracles, and I am still standing as a result of that – and the journey has not ended yet.

I feel like God is saying that there is so much more that he has for me, things He wants me to do, and it is just about getting a glimpse of it. If I could grasp a small part of what God can see, it would almost knock me off my feet to step into the things he has for me.

So my message is about stepping out of the box, because one big lesson that God has taught me on my journey is, "Don't limit me!" I believe we limit God by what we *think* He can do in a circumstance, or when we think, "How can He possibly do this?" We use our own understanding to try and put Him in a box, specifying how He can solve a certain problem; but God wants us to step outside the box and actually see Him in His glory and how big He is. Only then can we have a concept that nothing is impossible. *Nothing is impossible at all.* For me, that is what I stand for on my journey. My journey is still in progress and God is still on His throne.

There are things on the horizon that God is also challenging me about. I have always been known as a singer throughout my life because I come from quite a musical background. All my siblings either sing or play a musical instrument. We have been involved in worship and gospel music all our lives. But I believe that God wants me to expand into other areas. So this is not the end but just the beginning. There are many more things to come, I believe, lots and lots more! My only prayer is that everything I do will bring glory to God: "...not my will, but yours be done." (Luke 22:42)

Onwards and upwards!

GAIL JACKSON

Age:	*39*
Family:	*Married with three children*
Started at Ivy:	*1998*
Choice of beverage:	*Cortado – short and strong*

I grew up in a Christian family. My parents became Christians when we were very young. They had occasionally attended their local Church of Scotland, which was very dour and serious. Then a new minister came who was a charismatic Christian and a radical man of God. He started house groups and we became part of a house church. I became a Christian at the age of five, I believe, and I grew up with a strong church life. My parents were evangelical Christians and I was always aware of spiritual matters from a young age. I have been a Christian for thirty-five years now.

I was a mediocre Christian for a long time. Through my teenage years, like most people, I wavered slightly but I never totally rebelled. I knew that faith was definitely something I would have to choose myself at some point but I think I always lived by the law of Christianity. My morals were Christian, which isn't easy when you are away at university; I stuck to my principles and always felt protected by having those strong morals about relationships and not making certain choices that other people were making.

Yet I did not have the brilliant part of Christianity; my spiritual life was not great. It was as if I was living under the law – although not through fear; I was living by grace but just not in the fullness of Christ. I stuck with church and enjoyed it, and I had a relationship with Jesus, but I felt guilty that something wasn't completely right.

If I think about the real turning points, the first was that my friend who was having a difficult time did a course called Freedom in Christ and it really transformed her – quite amazingly. As a close group of Christian young women, we were all much the same, plodding a bit and talking about how we did not like ourselves, you know? We wished we were this and we wished we were that, and we weren't living in the freedom that God offers.

I started the Freedom in Christ course and found it very challenging. In fact, I had to stop! The sessions about breaking strongholds and recognising the quiet voice that tells you you're not worth anything or just feeds you little lies were too close to home. I was insecure about a lot of things and I didn't feel my value – although I was in a happy home situation. It wasn't that anything was bad on the outside, but I had confidence issues.

The Freedom in Christ course really resonated with me. Although I had to stop, I tried again and found it very helpful. I recommend everyone who is a Christian to do this course, no matter how long they have been following Jesus.

Now I want to carry this – to be an encourager of other people and also my own children. Although I grew up in a Christian home, and it was a loving Christian home, I did not experience being empowered regarding who I am in Christ, based on the promises of God.

I was made redundant when I had my third child, which was a bonus because I had four years at home and had time to get more involved with church activities. I was able to start leading at Ivy Toddlers and set up Messy Church.

I always knew I should get baptised but I hate being up front and 'on show' so the thought of it terrified me. If you have been a Christian for a long time, people just assume you are baptised so I just kept my head down! However, two years ago I felt convicted that I should be obedient and just do it. I was so scared that I could hardly talk but I am so glad I did it.

There was an Ivy conference a few years back called 'Keys to the City', with Graham Cooke. A lot of what he said was about identity and not waiting for things to change; instead we proclaim the truth already now. We don't always have to 'pray things in' because it's already been done, and we can get ourselves tangled up in things that are not actually true. He talked about us having the 'keys to the city'. It is obvious and so true that God has already given us the strength to do what he asks us and given us everything that we need. The key thing I remembered was, "If you've ever been given prophetic scriptures, go back to them and ask God what they mean to you."

When my husband and I got married, a wise friend gave us Proverbs 31:8-9:

> *Speak up for those who cannot speak for themselves, for the rights of all who are destitute. Speak up and judge fairly; defend the rights of the poor and needy.*

I always thought that word was for my husband, as he worked for Tearfund overseas and now for a children's charity. I thought that my role was to support him in his work, but years later, when I went back to those verses, I had one of those 'Holy Spirit moments' and I realised, "That's for me! That's for me too!"

I went to a conference called G&T for women at Ivy. I was surrounded by inspiring ladies. I wrote down the passions God had given me and one of them was "helping the poor". Around the same time, Ivy opened a Christians Against Poverty (CAP) debt centre and the talk that Matt Barlow from CAP gave one Sunday really 'blew me away'. I volunteered for CAP when my youngest child started playgroup and I loved it. It was another Holy Spirit moment when I read that one of CAP's key verses is Proverbs 31:8-9; it just made me cry.

As part of the children's work, Dave Hill was encouraging the leaders and so we did a course called 'Story Line'. It was about plotting your life story and seeing how God was involved in it and that if you want to get somewhere, you need to be specific about it and make certain decisions to get there. You have to identify how you will know when you have met your goal. That's when I realised that 'my thing' was not kids' work. I do it and I have children but it has not been the thing most on my heart. My greatest desire was to become a debt coach for Christians Against Poverty and my dream scenario would be to start the training – that would be my absolute goal.

When I started volunteering for CAP, someone said to me that a debt coach must first and foremost be an evangelist. I thought, "Oh, no!" as I have always been a bit of a chicken! But I also thought, "Right, what steps do I need to take to be able to get to my goal?" I knew I needed to become brave and be an evangelist.

I had an amazing experience at Messy Church. Some mums from school came and I felt led to pray with one of them. I was terrified and very far out of my comfort zone. She is an amazing lady and over the next six months she started coming to Ivy. We went to Alpha together and she became a Christian and was baptized.

God's timing is so good because the CAP Centre Manager was looking for a replacement and my youngest child was just about to start school. It was my first job application and interview for eleven years. It included role play – not my strong point! A few years earlier I would not have had the C.V. for it and I could not have answered some of the questions in the application, such as, "Have you pioneered anything?" I had set up Messy Church (not that I had set out to do so for the job, but it had just happened). They asked, "Have you worked with other volunteers in a church capacity?" Yes, I had done Toddlers. And, "Have you led anyone to Christ recently?" Oh, yes! Yes, I had done one of those!

I went to training at CAP three weeks later and as I stood there inside the door it felt like a dream scenario. It was the first time in my life that I was actually doing what I had confidence that God wanted me to do – and I love it! If you would have told me I would be doing this job a few years ago, I would have fallen over laughing, as I'm a bit of a 1950s housewife and my husband does all the money side of things because he's really good at it! The job is daunting and I feel out of my comfort zone often but it forces me to rely on God. I love seeing people set free from debt, praying for people who may never have had someone pray with them before, and offering them hope.

Onwards and upwards!

SARAH ANNE SMALL

Age:	*32 (at time of interview)*
Family:	*Married with one son*
Started at Ivy:	*2001*
Choice of beverage:	*Normally a cup of tea. Today a*
	Decaf Cappuccino (a treat!)

I've got a lovely Christian mum and dad who own and run a farm in North Yorkshire. I was taken to church my whole life. It was quite a small Methodist chapel and I had one other friend who was a Christian my age; it seemed like everyone else was either a little child or an old lady.

For many years I just went along as it was the thing to do. Then in my teenage years, especially the early years, I started to wonder whether it was real or not, what was behind it. I started to ask questions about 'authentic lifestyle' – whether we really believed all that we said we did, why life didn't look a lot different, and how could you reconcile this transformational God with an apparently normal lifestyle. I became rather disenfranchised with church and there wasn't much for us teenagers.

So I decided that I didn't believe any of it – quite a head decision. I couldn't reconcile any of it, so I thought it was all fairy tales and nonsense. I would have quite liked to stop going to church, but that wasn't really an option because my parents said, "No!" and they're not for fighting. So I kept going along.

Then, when I was about sixteen or seventeen, I went to a Christian Theatre Summer School for a week. There was a girl there who was my age who was a Christian. She kept going on about her relationship with God, like it was real. *It's not real, it's all made up. Why do you think it's real when you are my age?* It gave me food for thought: that people my age do accept this; it's not just a grown-up thing or an old person's thing.

A year or so later my best friend, who was my only friend in church, had gone on a Soul Survivor camp. When she came back she was adamant that she'd become a Christian, she'd met God and she'd had an amazing religious experience, weeping and all the rest of it. I was really 'gutted'; I was very disappointed. "No! No! You're not allowed to become a Christian. You're my friend and we're supposed to be sceptical together."

I got invited to join a Christian Union at school but I interrupted, "I think you should probably know that I am not actually a Christian!"

"Oh, we thought you were – because you go to church."

"Err... no!" I shrugged.

Not long after I said that, I did start to think. I read some books and went along to Soul Survivor myself. I used to go and listen to the World Wide Message Tribe, Y Friday and various other Christian bands. I liked that lifestyle but it still didn't link up in my head.

I can't quite remember how the penny dropped but I was reading a book from The Chronicles of Narnia in bed. It was The Last Battle, which is all about the end of things. There was a big battle which came to a head and Aslan called the children into a new world. Everything that had gone before was nothing compared to this amazing new thing that was about to come. It put everything into perspective for me and suddenly I thought, "Well if this matters and it's real, and my friends are experiencing this stuff, then perhaps I need to make a decision for it. So tentatively, quietly in my room one night, I said, "OK, I'll give you a try, God." I was bargaining!

That was the start of it, a hesitant start of the journey, trying to read the Bible more. I had some great friends at school. Then in 2001 I went to Manchester to study Religion and Theology. I picked that subject just because I had always thought that religion was interesting and important; it motivated people to do things, and the things it motivated people to do were immense – from very positive to very negative.

When I came to university I joined Ivy. I did not fully engage, and lived a student lifestyle for three years, but towards the end I signed up to do an Alpha course. I think it was through that and through being in a group with people who really believed in it and took it seriously that I started to get back to my own personal journey in discovering who God was. I started praying and started to sift out the kind of behaviour that was hypocritical, and started to get more into God's Word.

I started to experience the Holy Spirit as well. That had always been a challenge, but people said they knew God or they felt God and I questioned, "How? You can't see Him. He's not physically there!" Then I started to 'feel' God and started speaking in tongues. It started to become exciting. I developed a passion to explore God more. I was beginning to realise that the only thing that would make a difference to the world was God, and people coming to know Him.

I started doing some voluntary work in Zambia after I'd graduated. Then I went back to do a Master's in Politics, thinking that if I could master Religion and Politics, I would have keys to all the problems of the world – which I didn't; I just ended up a bit jaded. Next I did a lot of voluntary work, helping a friend set up a charity. So I've been involved in charitable works since I left university, mainly because I think I've always wanted to be involved where church makes a practical difference to people's lives. Some of it has been great, other bits have been frustrating, but I've learned lots of things along the way.

I was involved with Alpha for a long time at church, running the courses. I helped in leading it and putting together talks etc. The first ever sermon I preached was awful. But Ivy is such a wonderful church that it gives you the opportunity to actually develop those gifts. We had some great people behind us like Debra Green and Lynn Swart and all those who championed us young ladies and leaders of the future, which was really encouraging and a great blessing.

Steve and I met at Ivy, and got to know each other much better on our first mission trip to Zambia. After eighteen months of long distance dating we married and moved to our first house in Wythenshawe.

We hoped that we could get involved in the community and be a positive influence. But I think we really struggled because it was just the two of us and there was no structure around us; there was nothing particular that we could plug in to. We were both working and too busy, so the idea didn't materialise into anything.

But after we married we had received a prophecy that we would have five to seven years of zigzagging. We took this to mean trips back and forth to different African countries because we were doing quite a lot of work every summer in Africa. We would do something and come home. We worked separately until we would find the community of our calling.

We thought the community might be in Kenya or at least somewhere in Africa, so we went over there for a while. It was an amazing experience, learning all about community development and people's faith. But we realised that as total outsiders we were not necessarily the most useful people to be there long-term. So we invested what we could in the team there, tried to bless them and then came back home.

Soon after, we had a chat with Anthony Delaney and Andy Hawthorne, who said that they were interested in Ivy getting more involved in the marginalised community. Up until then it had been quite a middle class church, which attracted lots of people but did not always have particular links with the community.

I was really excited about working with the Eden Network and moving on to an estate where we could make a difference. We started to pray about where that would be and had some ideas. I found myself bargaining with God again, saying, "Well, I don't want to live in the inner city because there are no trees and I don't want to live here because..." Being brought up on a farm I like some greenery in my life.

So when we first heard about Merseybank, I thought, "This is too good to be true; it is really nice round here." Then you peel back the layers and you see that it's not as nice as it first appears. There were a series of meetings, calls and invitations, and God decided that that was the place; we agreed and moved in three and a half years ago.

That has been another process of learning and growing to depend on God and I'm amazed, actually, at what he's done in that place. It's where we got our first house. It's where we eventually had our son Gideon after a process of waiting. He's been a real blessing as well; he's opened up so many doors for me personally, which means at the moment that I've got a strange role as itinerant friend, evangelist, pastor, pray-er – many things to many people. With a child in tow you can get through any door, pretty much.

One of the other things that happened when we got back from Kenya was that Anthony asked if I wanted to be part of the eldership of the church. I thought he was joking. I laughed at him and then I realised he *wasn't* joking; he was being quite serious. It was a massive honour to be recognised as someone who really loves Ivy and wants to help lead it further on. I planned to refuse and I went to tell him, but he ignored my refusal.

And that's been a process, really, of stepping up; the challenges in that role are huge, as is the responsibility, so it makes you grow and develop because you need to – for the sake of this amazing, big thing that you are invested in. At the moment life is a happy place. I love the church, love the estate, love my little man.

I'm in a strange middle ground at the moment because I've not done paid work for about eighteen months. Obviously, having Gideon has been quite life-consuming. Even so, I started doing a Master's in Theology last September because I thought I wanted to do something which was additional to childcare, something which was really interesting to me. And I feel that there's a reason for me doing that. I love it and I'm definitely being challenged. Occasionally I have a desire to write, to teach and so on, and I think the Master's is partly preparation for that, but what it will actually look like in the future is hard to say.

Life is more of a challenge now because I'm not just a one-man band. Everything I do has to fit in with Steve and Gideon and where we live. Yet I think that whatever I do, going forward, will link somehow to seeing people change, being transformed.

Onwards and upwards!